Knowing China

by

Gregory C. Chow
Princeton University, USA

NEW JERSEY • LONDON • SINGAPORE • SHANGHAI • HONG KONG • TAIPEI • CHENNAI

Published by

World Scientific Publishing Co. Pte. Ltd.

5 Toh Tuck Link, Singapore 596224

USA office: Suite 202, 1060 Main Street, River Edge, NJ 07661

UK office: 57 Shelton Street, Covent Garden, London WC2H 9HE

British Library Cataloguing-in-Publication Data
A catalogue record for this book is available from the British Library.

KNOWING CHINA

ISBN 981-238-673-4
ISBN 981-238-679-3 (pbk)

Printed in Singapore by Mainland Press

To

Milton Friedman

Paul Samuelson

Zhao Ziyang

from whom I have learned economics

About the Author

The author is Class of 1913 Professor of Political Economy and Professor of Economics, Emeritus, at Princeton University. He attended Cornell University (BA, 1951) and the University of Chicago (MA, 1952, and Ph.D., 1955). He was Assistant Professor and Associate Professor at MIT and Cornell University respectively before becoming a Research Staff member and Manager of Economic Research at the IBM Thomas J. Watson Research Center, from 1962 to 1970.

Between 1970 and 1997, He was the Professor of Economics and Director of the Econometric Research Program at Princeton University. In 2001, the Program was renamed the Gregory C. Chow Econometric Research Program in his honor.

Professor Chow has advised top government officials in Taiwan and mainland China. His previous books include *Demand for Automobiles in the United States: A Study in Consumer Durables* (1957); *Analysis and Control of Dynamic Economic Systems* (1975); *Econometrics* (1983); *The Chinese Economy* (1985); *Understanding China's Economy* (1994); *Asia in the Twenty-first Century* (1997); *Dynamic Economics: Optimization by the Lagrange Method* (1997) and *China's Economic Transformation* (2002).

Preface

The September 22, 2003 issue of *Financial Times* carried a major article with the title "Why Europe was the past, the US is the present and a China-dominated Asia the future of the global economy" [sentence added at page proof]. China has gained large economic and political influence in the world but few outsiders know it well. It is the main purpose of this book to fill the gap. China has an intriguing and fascinating history. Its culture makes the Chinese people talented and resourceful. Its economy is capitalistic and not as poor as many imagine it to be; it will overtake the US economy in total output in about 2020. It does not have a population problem; in fact, there are advantages in having a large population. It does not have a well developed legal system in Western style but has a moral-legal system that works if one knows the rule of doing business. The Chinese education system has strengths as well as weaknesses. Science is quite advanced and there is a high-tech explosion in China. The Chinese people are quite happy and free. Its government officials are capable people, and the government has done a lot for the people in the last 25 years, after having made serious mistakes in the two decades before. Most Chinese support their government. Shanghai and Hong Kong are very dynamic modern cities. In many ways, Shanghai is more advanced than New York, as former Treasury Secretary Robert Rubin remarked in a speech in Princeton on March 28, 2003. China has many interesting places for tourists to visit. The country is like a large park or museum. Partnership with China is good for the United States in assuming its world leadership. The above themes will be elaborated upon in this book as it guides the reader through the many facets of China that he needs to know.

People who have traveled to China in recent years realize that China is a remarkable country in many ways and are likely to agree with most of what I have to say. People who intend to visit China for the first time will find this book useful. For the remaining residents in the United States and the rest of the Western world, the presence of China will be increasingly felt in their daily lives as more Chinese products appear in their home markets, more business opportunities in China become available and recognized, more Chinese travel elsewhere and as the US government will be more involved with China in assuming its leadership role in the community of nations.

Having spent my early years in China, until the completion of my freshman year in 1948, I was first exposed to a Chinese way of thinking. Much of that thinking has been modified and integrated in the last 55 years of living in the United States. As an economist, I tend to think in economic terms. Economic thinking has affected my way of looking at other subjects such as culture, as can be seen in the beginning of Chapter 2 for example. Economists appreciate the working of the invisible hand, often side with the market rather than the government, and prefer freedom to government intervention, provided that law and order is assured. As an academic, I have published 11 other books, most of them academic. This is the first book that I have written mainly for the general reader, although I would not object if some professors assign it for their courses. I am also a realist and do not think like a typical academic in many ways partly because I worked for IBM for eight wonderful years, and partly because I had to deal with real-life economic and political problems.

I have become more of a realist after serving as an advisor to leaders and top government officials in Taiwan from the 1960s onward and in Mainland China from the 1980s. I am still active in both areas, interacting with people in the governments, in business and in educational and research institutions. Since the early 1980s I have taken two to three trips per year to mainland China/Hong Kong/Taiwan, spending a total of six to eight weeks per year. In discussing China I am not only an observer, but also a member of its community. As a result I have learned a great deal about China, some from working experience with top and middle-level government officials as discussed in Chapter 6.

The content of this book is easily seen from the titles of the nine chapters in it. Chapter 1 can be read first. The remaining chapters can be read in any order according to the interest of the reader. Each chapter will provide some general information as well as my own insights on the topic concerned.

In writing this book I am indebted to many persons. When only the first draft of several chapters was completed I circulated it to and received helpful suggestions from Gary Becker, James Chow, Peter Dougherty, Paula Duffy, Wen Fong, Milton Friedman, Bruce Gilley, Michael Intrilligator, Susan Solomon, Jack Tchen and Robert Venturi. For the later drafts of the manuscript, I have received helpful comments from Paula Chow, Hu Shouwei, Harvey Lam, Jianping Mei, Ivan Png and Pei Zhu. To all of them I would like to express my sincere thanks without implying that any of them necessarily agrees with the views expressed herein which are my own. The excellent work of Ms. Ho Sheo Be and Ms. Amy Liu in editing and translating the manuscript respectively is much appreciated.

Gregory C. Chow
Princeton, NJ
July 2003

Contents

List of Figures

Some Facets of China's History

Knowing China requires some knowledge of its history. Since Chinese history is a broad and difficult subject, I can only provide some facets of it that seem to me most relevant and interesting. In particular, I will emphasize those aspects of China's historical heritage that affect the present-day China. China is an important country because it has 1.3 billion people and the Chinese can draw on the historical heritage to enrich their lives. It was relatively a very rich country in 1700. It produced many highly valued products that were exported to the West, first through the Silk Route and later across the oceans. It had more books than the rest of the world combined. After more than one hundred years of relative decline since 1840, it has recovered much of its previous position in the world community. I will elaborate on this story below.

Shang, 1766–1121 BC — Advanced Culture and Rich Human Resources

China has a recorded history of over 4,000 years, beginning with or before the Shang dynasty. The Chinese culture was advanced during the Shang dynasty. There was a written language as seen in the engravings on turtle shells. Some historians define history narrowly to include only what has been recorded, but even by this narrow

(Smile)

(Cry)

(Characters by Gregory Chow)

definition the events recorded on turtle shells qualify Shang as a historical period. People told fortunes by first writing on the shells and then seeing where the cracks appeared after they burned the shells. This "oracle" language was in the form of symbols. It later evolved into characters used in the Chinese written language. The symbols or characters representing the sun, the moon, people and other objects simple to draw are obvious and understandable to anyone. The present-day characters for smile and crying are still distinguishable even by people not knowing the language. One looks like a smiling face, and the other a crying face (please see facing page). Bronze vessels from the Shang dynasty exhibited in museums show how advanced technology and art were at the time.

Zhou, 1122–211 BC — Golden Period of Development of Chinese Thoughts

Mathematics was already fairly advanced in the Zhou dynasty in 1100 BC as imbedded in *Yiching, The Book of Changes*. This book can be found in most American bookstores. Besides *Yiching*, other books of the Zhou period were impressive, including the *Book of Poems*, the *Book of Learning*, the *Book of Li (Rules of Social Conduct)*, and *Spring and Autumn (History of the Late Zhou Period)*. There were many great thinkers during this period. Among them Confucius (551–479 BC) was the most celebrated. He is considered the originator of Chinese humanism. He established moral codes to guide human conduct, and a set of proper relations among different members of a society, between emperor and subjects, parents and children, older and younger brothers, and husband and wife. We will have more to say about Confucianism in Chapter 2 dealing with Chinese culture and in Chapter 3 dealing with the Chinese economy.

Besides Confucius, there were many other prominent philosophers. There was Lao Tse who was the founder of Daoism, advocating the return to nature and "doing nothing in following the course of nature." Lao Tse suggested that if there are no laws, there will be no laws to break and there will be no criminals. There was Han Fei-tze who taught almost the opposite by emphasizing the importance of the legal system. There was Guan Zhong who understood much economics including the incentives of different forms of government taxation. There were a hundred schools of thought contending, like a hundred flowers blooming and a hundred birds singing. It was a golden period of China's cultural development. The writings of that period are available today for us to read and enjoy.

Qin, 200 BC — National Unification and Strong Government

At the end of Zhou dynasty, many states rivaled for power. This is known as the Period of Warring States. Among them were seven strong ones. These states came about because the emperors of Zhou annexed territories to relatives and imperial officials for them to govern. These people gradually declared themselves kings of independent states. After much fighting and diplomatic maneuvering, the emperor of the state of Qin became the victor in 200 BC. Not only was his state strong, his army powerful and his ability as a leader truly exceptional, he also knew how to play one of the other six states off against another and broke the alliance once formed by them. Historians have blamed some of the other six states for appeasing Qin, but the military power and skillful diplomacy of the latter also contributed to its success. The victorious Qin emperor declared himself the First Emperor as he was anticipating many more emperors to come in his dynasty.

The performance of the First Emperor of Qin was impressive, though not necessarily moral. He was a very strong and able leader, skillful both in administration and in military and diplomatic affairs. He used highly developed armaments as now displayed in the Museum of Xi'an. Xi'an is the city where the world famous models of the Qin terracotta soldiers were buried in the tomb of the First Emperor. The tomb is about 1.5 kilometers in diameter. The several thousand soldiers are only guards of its entrance, a small part of the tomb. Since afterlife was considered more important than this life, much effort was made to construct the tomb for the emperor to enjoy his afterlife. Its construction was so complicated and intricate that with modern technology and much resource at its disposal, the current Chinese government has not found itself capable of excavating the main parts of the tomb. It is believed that the interior of the tomb is protected in such a way as to make it very difficult for intruders to get in without getting hurt or destroying the treasures inside.

The Qin Emperor succeeded in unifying the country as one political entity and unifying the written language and the system of weights and measures. Realizing the danger of decentralization by allowing too much power to the regional aristocrats, he centralized the administration by placing the regional and local governors under the control of the central government. One of the main criticisms of his rule was that he ordered the burning of many books and the burial of many dissenting scholars alive. The freedom of expression was curtailed. To his credit he also built, or connected, large sections of the Great Wall to protect China from invasion. The name China originates from the word "Qin" as pronounced much like "chin."

Han, 206 BC–220 AD — Large Empire and Adoption of Confucianism; a Great Historian

The empire of Qin did not last long. A well-known Chinese classical essay examining the fault of Qin attributes its downfall to its authoritarian rule and failure to treat the people with kindness. After the death of the First Emperor, his son, the second emperor to be, was unable to rule. There came two powerful leaders of the states of Chu and Han. Their contention for the throne was so well remembered in China that the two sides of a Chinese chessboard are named after them. Chu started out as the much stronger of the two but finally lost to Han, which became the Han dynasty (206 BC–220 AD). The Chu leader was in a position to eliminate the leader of Han. In fact one evening he invited the Han leader for dinner with a plan to kill him. Dancing was staged at the dinner. Once the Chu host gave the signal, the dancer with a sword would kill the Han leader. There were only four persons at the dinner, with one advisor or assistant for each leader. When the dance advanced to the point for the Chu leader to give the signal, he made no movement. His advisor who helped stage the dinner was greatly disappointed, sighing that the kingdom was lost!

How did this happen? The story was written up in a few short sentences in the *Records of the Historian*, perhaps the greatest history book of China, written by the historian Sima Qian of the Han dynasty. Professor of History Yu Ying-shi of Princeton University wrote an article interpreting the few sentences of Sima. The article (Yu, 1981, pp. 184–195, in Chinese) is entitled "Explicating the Seating Arrangement of the Hongmen Banquet." I was much impressed by this article, for its recognition that the seating arrangement of the four persons present determined Chinese history as described in a few simple sentences of Sima. The passage has only 60 Chinese characters in total to describe the entire event, including all four major actors and what happened. Every word was properly chosen. Every sentence is simple and precise. Without stealing from the perceptive and interesting discussion of the article, let me just relate the gist of the story. The advisor of the Han leader was wise enough to ask him to take the seat befit of a servant, to the point that the Chu leader considered the position as a sign of surrender and saw no need to kill him. In China, then and now, the position of a seat at a dinning table in terms of the direction it faces is important to distinguish the position of its occupant. Professor Yu has explicated this passage and illustrated the simplicity, clarity and depth of Sima's writing.

To give the reader a taste of the wisdom and the literary skill of Sima, let me cite one passage. This passage came to my attention from Young (1996, p. 138) who quoted from the chapter entitled "The Biographies of the Money Markets" in Sima's *Records of the Historian*.

"There must be farmers to produce food, men to extract the wealth of mountains and marshes, artisans to produce these things and merchants to circulate them. There is no need to wait for government orders: each man will play his part, doing his best to get what he desires. So cheap goods will go where they will fetch more, while expensive goods will make men search for cheap ones. When all work willingly at their trade, just as water flows ceaselessly downhill day and night, things will appear unsought and people will produce them without being asked. For clearly this accords with the Way and is in keeping with nature."

This remarkable passage shows that Sima understood the working of a free market economy some 1,800 years before the publication of Adam Smith's *Wealth of Nations* in 1776. He understood the economic law of supply and demand based on people trying to do the best for themselves, and economic coordination achieved by an "invisible hand" without government planning. One wishes that the Chinese economic planners in the 1950s to the 1970s had read and understood this passage. It also shows that China had a well functioning market economy at the time.

Han's economy was quite developed. There was trade not only with the people in the North but also people in the West through the Silk Route and thus trade indirectly with people in Europe. Han emperors tried to achieve a stable government by adopting the teaching of Confucius to rule. Confucianism assigns roles to different members of society. Children should respect and obey their parents. Friendship should be based on honesty, trust and mutual respect. Ministers should serve the emperor, and lower-level administrators should yield to higher-level ones. The emperor has the right to rule over the entire population but only if he treats them properly and follows certain basic principles of good government. By misconduct an emperor can lose his right to rule or the mandate of Heaven. To aspire to move upward socially, a person first disciplines himself, then learns how to act as the head of his family, then to rule his country and finally to govern the entire world in peace. This particular teaching was mainly aimed at men, although there were woman emperors in Chinese history. The positions of men and women were not equal, but the assigned roles provided social stability for many years. In a family, the wife should follow or sing to the tune of the husband, but the husband should love and respect his wife. Not all of Confucius' teaching is applicable to the Chinese society today, but in my opinion its basic ideas for individual conduct and social harmony still are.

In order to remain influential, Confucianism needs to be adapted to the conditions of present day life in China. All surviving religions in the world have to be adapted to changing circumstances. The same applies to Confucianism even though Confucianism is not a religion in the sense of believing in God. Confucius proclaimed that he did not have much to say about God. Confucian ethics still has a strong influence on the life of the Chinese today. Some people think that its influence is mostly a hindrance to economic progress. I tend to believe that its positive influence outweighs its negative influence. Through Confucian ethics, the Chinese people have learned to be honest, to work hard, to be loyal to their friends and to work for the good of the society. There are two important points that I will discuss further in Chapter 3 dealing with the Chinese economy and in Chapter 6 dealing with the Chinese government. The first is that although China does not have a well-functioning modern (Western) legal system, business can be conducted in an orderly manner on the basis of the ethical and moral principles of Confucius. The Chinese are taught that good moral behavior is more important than simply obeying laws that may not be ethical. This has enabled the Chinese market economy to function all through the history, especially during the Song period in about 1100 when China had a flourishing market economy. The second is that the Chinese consider responsibility more important than freedom (at least relatively more important, as compared with the view of most Americans) and the common good of the society as a whole more important than an individual's self interests when the two are in conflict. It is good to sacrifice oneself to serve the society. As President John F Kennedy once appealed to fellow Americans, "Ask not what your country can do for you, but what you can do for your country."

Three Kingdoms, 220–80; Jin, 265–420; and Succession of Dynasties, 304–589

At the end of Han was the period of Three Kingdoms. As the name suggests, there were then three kingdoms contending to succeed Han to form a new dynasty. The history of this period was written in the *Record of Three Kingdoms*. A novel *The Romance of Three Kingdoms*, written by Luo Guanzhong, was based partly on the historical record. The novel is a very popular and exciting book for children and adults alike. It is a book of strategies, in war and in love affairs. A contemporary Chinese politician or diplomat can benefit from studying the strategies in the book, provided that she maintains her moral character. There are strategies for both offense and defense. Since there are three parties, any one can play the second against the third. This happened many times in the novel, and in actual history. The available strategies in a competition involving three parties are much more interesting and complicated than in a competition between only two. Perhaps there is something in the novel for the game theorists of today to study, although I have not thought much about the stories from the perspective of game theory.

One of the kingdoms finally won, after many interesting turns of events. The Jin dynasty was established, lasting from 265–420 AD. Because of the invasions of the nomadic people from the north, the country became fragmented. A succession of dynasties lasted from 304–589 AD. In spite of the political disunity, or perhaps because of the wars, there was progress in technology, including the invention of the gunpowder and the wheelbarrow and the improvement of Chinese medicine during the later part of this period.

Tang, 618–901 — Trade, Buddhism and Poetry

Unification was achieved by the short-lived Sui dynasty (581–617). The rule of Sui was known to be harsh, with many laborers drafted to reconstruct the Great Wall and to build the Grand Canal going from south to north. A system of civil service examinations was introduced to select scholars well versed in Confucian classics to become government officials. Sui was succeeded by the glorious Tang dynasty (618–901). Tang was known for many great achievements. The Chinese people were also called the Tang people. Chinatowns in America today are still called the "Streets of the Tang People" in Chinese. The tri-colored Tang Horses made of clay are exhibited in art museums and admired by many.

Buddhism from India began to gain popularity in China during the Tang period. When trade with the West was flourishing, worshipers commissioned colorful religious paintings on the walls inside the caves along the Silk Route. These are among the art treasures of the world. For the Chinese, Tang poetry was the most appreciated achievement of this period. A book of 300 best known poems written by Tang poets can be found in every Chinese home, even if there is a collection of only a small number of books. The best-loved poems are simple, conveying an interesting or emotionally moving message. They are easy to memorize and rhyme beautifully. There are so many good poems for an ordinary educated Chinese to recite that even those who cannot read can recite a few popular ones.

One long poem tells the love story of a Tang emperor and his concubine. He spent so much time with her as to ignore the affairs of the state. A rebellion occurred and had to be suppressed, but the army did not want to fight unless he got rid of the concubine. He was forced to order the termination of her life, only to regret deeply after the rebellion was suppressed. The name of the poem is "Forever Sorrow" or "Everlasting Regret." On the one hand, a historian might point out the incompetence of the emperor and his negligence of the affairs of the state for the love of a woman, and consider his love affair improper. On the other , the poem arouses so much emotion, tenderness and sympathy on the part of the reader that only the enduring love on the part of a noble emperor is recognized without any thought of possible misconduct on his part. One can keep on reciting such a beautiful Tang poem and repeat it many times, each time with more understanding and deeper emotions.

Song, 960–1126 — A Flourishing Capitalist Economy

Song dynasty also had its beautiful poems, although of different forms from Tang's. They are not made up of sentences of equal length, but have to fit into particular forms. They tend to be more romantic, dealing with the tragedy of love lost. Song suffered from invasions by people from the north, leading to the move of its capital city to the Southern city of Hangzhou along the Yangtze River. Song has its share of poets, scholars, calligraphers, painters, and statesmen. Song is also known for its highly developed market economy.

When I teach a course on the Chinese economy at Princeton I sometimes show how developed the Song economy was by showing a well-known painting "Along the River during the Qingming Festival." There are different versions of this painting, or similar paintings of this title. All show economic activities along the river. In the painting one can find restaurants, shops, and transportation by carts and boats, as well as people working, having leisure activities and trading. One can call the economy of Song a capitalist economy, although it differs from a modern capitalist economy as it lacks modern technology. An interesting question is why science and technology did not develop during the Song period. China had much scientific knowledge during that period, including mathematics and astronomy in particular. The state of scientific developments is documented by Joseph Needham (1956).

A plausible explanation can be found in China's social and economic structure. Scholars well versed in Chinese classics and government officials were accorded the highest position and commanded the highest respect in ancient Chinese society. Official positions were obtained by passing examinations on Chinese classics. Merchants and businessmen were not accorded a high social status in a Confucian society while money and wealth often came with government official positions. This social structure did not provide much incentive to study science, which was not taught to the children. Knowledge of Confucian classics and elegant calligraphy were more important. Furthermore, the economic advantage of technological innovation was limited because of the abundance of low-cost and high-quality labor. For an innovation to be economically viable it had to be capable of producing the same product at a lower cost than using labor. When an innovation was introduced the initial cost was high. It was only after much improvement and when the economy of large-scale production set in that the economic use of technology could replace China's cheap labor. The above two sets of considerations may explain partially why science and technology did not develop in China during the Song dynasty and later periods. They may not provide an entirely satisfactory explanation to some readers and even to me. The subject remains an interesting one for further study.

Yuan, 1279–1368 — Rule by Mongols but Han Culture Survived

Before the Yuan dynasty, Han people ruled China. Han refers to the majority ethnic group in China. At least from the Han dynasty onward, Mongols from the north tried to invade China repeatedly. They finally succeeded and established the Yuan dynasty in 1279. The founder was Hubilie, the grandson of Genghis Khan. Yuan was very strong militarily. Genghis Khan built a Mongolian empire, which extended all the way to Europe. In occupying and ruling China, the Mongolians absorbed the culture of the Han Chinese. In studying Chinese history, Chinese children in later periods were told that the Han Chinese culture was so resilient that although invaders could conquer and rule China, they had to learn the Han culture and rule by adopting the Han way of life. This happened again later in the Qing dynasty. The resilience of the Chinese culture enabled China to survive the Western impact of the 19th century.

To anticipate later discussions, the last survival test was much more difficult to pass because the Western impact in the 19th and 20th century was much stronger and occurred during a period when the Chinese government was extremely incompetent and weak. The Western and Japanese imperial powers invading China with modern technology were much stronger militarily than any other invaders, including the Mongols and the Manchus who founded the Qing dynasty. They also had advanced forms of social and political structure and administrative skill that could replace China's. The impact occurred during a period when the Qing dynasty was on the decline and the ruling emperors were incompetent. Furthermore the attempt to modernize China through orthodox Communism was a mistaken course to take. In spite of these three very negative factors, China has managed not only to survive but also regain its strong position. This can be attributed to the resiliency of the Chinese culture and civilization, as I shall explain more fully in the remainder of this book.

Ming, 1368–1644 — Overseas Explorations

Han people resumed their rule during the Ming dynasty. One distinction is the overseas expeditions during the period 1405–1433 led by Zheng He, a eunuch and confidante of the emperor of the Ming dynasty. According to Gavin (2003), on March 8, 1421 Zheng He sailed the largest fleet the world had ever seen from China. The fleet reached America 70 years before Columbus and circumnavigated the globe a century before Magellan. One of the areas explored was Taiwan, leading to an exodus of Chinese immigrants to this island. During the early period of the Qing dynasty that followed Ming, the Han Chinese in Taiwan assisted in a rebellion in the mainland to overthrow the rulers of the Qing dynasty. This was a part of Chinese history used by the current People's Republic of China's (PRC) government to base its claim that Taiwan is a part of China.

Qing, 1644–1911 — Impact of Western and Japanese Imperialism

During the later part of the Ming period, the government was weak and the throne was in danger. Not only was there an uprising by Han people, there were also invasions of the Mongolians from the North and the Manchus from the Northeast. After much struggle, the dynasty collapsed and the Manchus succeeded in ruling China and founded the Qing dynasty. The Qing emperors accepted the Han Chinese language as the official language and used the Han people to govern the country, although there was some mistrust of them as compared with the Manchu ministers. The early Qing emperors were very able and intelligent. Emperor Kangxi was a capable leader and administrator. Using Han people to serve in his government he established a strong government and expanded China's spheres of influence to neighboring countries. He was responsible for the compilation of a comprehensive dictionary which the Chinese still use today.

Bypassing the glorious years of Qing, I turn quickly to the 19th century when the Qing emperors were incompetent and the government was weak. It happened to be a high point of the British Empire. The Empire covered large areas in the continents of Africa, Europe, America, Asia and Australia. It included India, where economic power was exercised through the East India Company. Through this company, the British wanted to trade with China, as they desired Chinese goods such as porcelain, silk and especially tea. The British were consuming a large amount of tea at that time. To pay for the Chinese products they needed to export to China. The Chinese did not care much about the products that the British had to offer, except for opium. The Qing government wanted to stop the import of opium. The conflict of the two countries resulted in the Opium War of 1840. China was defeated. In the Treaty of Nanking signed in 1842, China not only gave up its right to prevent the import of opium, but was forced to give Hong Kong to the British and open its rivers for British shipping. China's government became even weaker following the defeat. The Chinese people were humiliated and angry at the British and the Qing government.

After the Opium War, other foreign powers obtained concessions from China through wars followed by a succession of unequal treaties. Controversies arose from attempts to open up Canton (now Guangzhou) to trade, resulting in a joint Anglo-French expedition against Peking in 1858. One consequence of this episode was the burning of the famous Yuan Ming Yuan, (the Summer Palace) a few miles west of the capital by the British and French troops. The Manchu government was compelled to sign the Treaty of Peking in 1860 and to give up further rights to both countries. A war with France ended with the signing of the treaty of Tientsin in 1885, conceding Vietnam as a French protectorate. Burma was seceded to the British in 1886. In 1897, Germany occupied Tsingtao, and obtained a lease of Kiaochow for 99 years. Similar leasing agreements were reached with Russia (for Dalian), Britain (Weihaiwei) and France (Kwangchowwan).

China's concessions included war indemnities, opening of city ports, surrendering of rights to inland water navigation and to railroad building, leasing of territories to foreign powers, and loss of territories formerly within China's sphere of influence as stated above. Areas in parts of Shanghai were leased to the British, the French and other foreign governments. Two of the most tragic events were the Sino-Japanese War of 1894-5 and the foreign invasion of 1900 after the Boxer Rebellion. Defeated in the Sino-Japanese War, China gave up Korea, a country formerly paying tribute to China, and Taiwan, a part of its territory. In reaction to the rebellion of the Boxers who had harmed foreigners, armies from eight countries (Britain, Russia, Germany, France, America, Italy, Austria and Japan, names that Chinese school children were told to memorize in history classes) invaded China and extracted indemnities from China after she was defeated. The American government later used a part of the war indemnity to support Chinese students to study in the United States. By the early 20th century many parts of China became semi-colonies of foreign powers.

Modernization became the dream of China's government and its people, and nationalism was aroused. Some government officials initiated what was known as the Hundred Days' Reform of the Qing government in 1898. It was supported by a weak and young emperor Guangxu but opposed by the strong Empress Dowager. The reformers were quite idealistic, but the reform movement was able to last only for 103 days. Other officials in the Qing government did not support the Hundred Days' Reform and preferred a more gradual reform, perhaps to establish a constitutional monarchy. A third group, outside the government, advocated a revolution to overthrow the Qing dynasty for its failure in dealing with the foreign invasions and in modernizing China. The fact that the rulers of Qing belonged to a minority ethnic group also weakened their support by the Han majority.

The Republic of China, 1911 — Political Disunity, Wars and Economic Progress

A revolution succeeded in 1911 when the Qing government was overthrown and the Republic of China was established. The revolution succeeded because the Qing government no longer received the support of the Chinese people, or even of its own army which yielded to the revolutionaries. The revolutionaries were not well organized. They attempted to overthrow the Qing government several times without success. Many of them were surprised when one attempt in Wuhan succeeded in 1911. Sun Yat-sen, the leader of the Guomindang, known as the Nationalist Party in the West, hurriedly returned from abroad to become its Temporary President. He had no command over the military and was not able to rule. Several months later Yuan Shikai, the prime minister in the Qing government, became the first President of China. He ruled for about four years and wanted to return the government to a monarchy and to assume the position of an emperor. This move did not receive the support of other government and military leaders and his attempt failed. He died soon after.

In the early years of the Republic of China the country was politically unstable. A few years after Yuan's death, the presidency changed hands several times. Changes in the premiership and in the composition of the cabinet members were more frequent, often due to the loss of support for the president who used his prime minister as the scapegoat. By support I do not mean popular support, but the support of the powerful military leaders. China was a republic only in name but not in substance. There was a parliament composed of members selected by provincial governments. The president was supposed to be elected by the members of parliament. If a president could not get sufficient votes from the parliament but had strong support of the military leaders or governors of important provinces, he could dissolve the parliament by claiming that it was illegitimately composed. With the support of enough provincial governors or military leaders he could organize and legitimize a new parliament to acquire sufficient votes. An important lesson to learn from studying the history of this period is that a democratic government cannot be established to function simply by setting up institutions in form. Democratic institutions can be established in name and in form but they may not function properly. This statement applies to political, legal, economic and other social institutions, as will be discussed later in this book.

In the years after Yuan's death in 1916, China was politically divided, between the north and the south and even among provinces in each region. There was a government in Beijing in the north, headed by a President. This presidency changed hands often as has been just described. There was no political unity even in northern China. Provincial governors and military leaders controlled their own territory. They yielded allegiance to the President in Beijing as they pleased. Only with sufficient support from them, a president in Beijing could actually rule northern China. In the South, provincial governors had even more independence. Sometimes they actually declared independence from any national government. Most of the time they were willing to be a part of the government of the north, or of the South. If there was a southern government at all, it would move from location to location. Guangzhou was one favorite location. After failing to be the President in Beijing, Sun Yat-sen tried to assume leadership in the South as President of a government located in Guangzhou. His leadership was often challenged by strong military leaders including members of his own Nationalist Party. Several times the northern and southern governments attempted to negotiate a settlement but never succeeded to form a union. China was a politically divided country.

In an attempt to assume leadership in China, Sun Yat-sen decided to cooperate with the Communist Party in the early 1920s. The Chinese Communist Party was founded in Shanghai in 1921 by a group of people who saw the formation of this party as providing the best solution to China's problem of modernization — the same goal with which the Chinese Nationalist Party had been founded. The establishment of the Soviet Union in 1921 provided many people feeling oppressed and deprived with hopes. Even many Americans experiencing or observing the Great Depression of the early 1930s accepted communism as a solution to the economic problems of the United States. Sun Yat-sen received little support from the western countries. By cooperating with the Chinese Communists, the Nationalist Party could be strengthened and obtain support from the Soviet Union. With support from the Soviet government and cooperation from members of the Communist Party Sun founded the Huangpu Military Academy along the Pearl River south of Guangzhou. Chiang Kai-shek was the head of the Academy, and Zhou Enlai served as director of the political department. After Sun's death in 1924, Chiang led a northern expedition in order to unify China.

Before we move on to the Northern Expedition, it is worth pointing out the role of intellectuals in political movements in China. In the historical tradition, Chinese scholars and intellectuals aspired to become government officials. They tried to compete in imperial examinations in order to be selected. By Confucian teachings, they were responsible for the prosperity and demise of the nation. Motivated further by the sense of nationalism and the desire to modernize China after the Opium War, the intellectuals became involved in political affairs. They formed the Nationalist Party and the Communist Party. When China was humiliated by the decisions of the Paris Peace Conference at the end of World War I, students in Beijing organized demonstrations to protest. One decision unfavorable to China, a country having fought on the winning side of the War, was the transfer of the city of Qingdao (Tsingtao) previously occupied by the defeated Germany to Japan instead of China. Recognizing the need for modernization, the students led the May 4 Movement in 1919 not only to protest against the policies of their weak government but to change the culture of the country for the purpose of mod ernization. Science and technology was championed. Democracy was embraced. Confucianism was under attack. Old traditions had to be reexamined. Some advocated a change in writing style from the literary style that had been practiced for over two thousand years to a modern style which corresponds more closely to the spoken language. Some intellectuals became active politically in the activities of the Nationalist Party or the Communist Party, while others asserted their influence by writing or teaching at universities. In spite of the political division and instability in the 1920s the intellectuals managed to generate new styles of literature and poetry and conduct original research in natural sciences, social sciences and humanities in an open and free academic environment.

Chiang Kai-shek led the Northern Expedition in 1926 with cooperation of the Communists. Soon after the armies reached Wuhan and Shanghai, two major cities along the Yangtze River, he parted with the Communists and staged the killing of many of them in Shanghai. In 1928, the Nationalist army trained in Huangpu reached Beijing, having defeated the armies of many provincial military leaders, called warlords in the language of the Nationalist press. Chiang proclaimed the unification of China, but the unification was partially nominal. The governors of several provinces, including those in the Northeast, declared allegiance to Chiang's national government, but they retained control of their own provinces and extracted concessions from Chiang. Under the circumstances, Chiang's effort was a remarkable achievement towards China's unification, but the degree of unification achieved was much lower than what Mao Zedong was to achieve later in 1949 when the People's Republic of China was founded.

From 1928 to 1949, China's history was characterized by three major wars. First was the war with Japan. Japan started invading the Northeastern provinces of China in 1930 and established a puppet government known as Manchuguo, with the deposed young Qing emperor as king. In 1937, Japan formally declared war against China and soon occupied much of China's coastal areas. Then came the Second World War for China when Japan attacked Pearl Harbor on December 8 (early morning China time, and early afternoon Eastern standard time on December 7) 1941. China joined the Allies and claimed victory over Japan on August 14, 1945. I have counted the Second World War separately as the second war for China during this period. The third was the civil war between the National government and the Communists.

Ever since the breaking up with the Communists in 1926, Chiang wanted to destroy the Communists. In 1933, the Nationalist army began chasing the Communists for several thousand miles without being able to destroy them. This was known as the Long March. The Communists, perhaps with only ten percent surviving, finally settled in the interior city of Yan'an. Chiang understood the danger of the Communists as a threat to his leadership and government. He said perceptively that the Japanese were a cancer of the skin but the Communists were a cancer of the heart. He wanted to defeat the Communists first before waging a war against the Japanese in spite of Japan's repeated aggressions in the 1930s. He was detained in the City of Xi'an by one of his generals who was in favor of cooperating with the Communists to fight the Japanese. The general forced him to commit to this policy before releasing him from Xi'an. This Xi'an Incident was considered an important turning point in the struggle between the Nationalists and the Communists.

The struggle resumed after the end of World War II. The Communists were better organized and they had the support of many Chinese people. They had done an effective job in governing Yan'an too. In the mean time, the Chiang government officials were corrupt. Many officials extracted money from citizens before returning to them their properties that were taken over by the Japanese. Some officials used state properties for their own benefits, such as diverting money and goods belonging to state-owned factories to their own pockets or for sale as their own. China experienced a run-away inflation as the government kept printing money to finance its large payroll and the war against the Communists. Millions of Chinese dollars only had the value of one American dollar. When the government instituted a currency reform early in 1949, it exchanged the new currency for the old at the rate of one to one million and forced the people to surrender their gold and foreign currency in exchange for the new currency. People were executed openly on the streets of Shanghai when they kept their gold and foreign currency. The new currency soon lost much of its value. In effect the government confiscated the wealth of Chinese citizens. The unpopularity of the government and the lack of will power on the part of Nationalist soldiers to fight the Communists resulted in the victory of the latter. It also led to the establishment of the People's Republic of China on October 1 1949, as proclaimed by Chairman Mao facing a great mass of people celebrating in Tiananmen Square in Beijing. Chiang moved his government to Taiwan. One and a half million people consisting of the military, government officials and their families, and other Chinese citizens went with him.

The People's Republic of China, 1949– Present — From a Planned to a Market Economy

The new government was able to take over and administer a very large country. Besides providing law and order, there were numerous tasks to perform. One was to stabilize the price level. In the Spring of 1950, as a student, I wrote a paper for a course at Cornell on Chinese inflation. I found that the new government was able to stop the very serious inflation within several months, and expressed much admiration. At that time I did not understand the quantity theory of money in economics sufficiently to realize that inflation can be stopped by controlling the supply of money. The government introduced a new currency, the Renminbi *yuan* (RMB), meaning People's currency. People could acquire the new currency by surrendering the old currency at a reasonable exchange rate to preserve the purchasing power of their money holdings. Inflation was soon put under control because there was no excessive printing of the RMB.

A land reform was carried out. Most farmers were happy when they obtained land ownership after land reform. Some landowners were very poorly treated when they were accused of wrongdoings by tenant farmers in mass meetings staged by the Communists. Many of them were convicted of crimes and were executed brutally. The capitalists were first promised the ownership and control of their factories and enterprises, only to be told later that the enterprises were to be state-owned and they could serve as managers under the direction of the state planning authority. The farmers owning their land at one time were soon organized into collectives with the pretext that such organizations would increase productivity. Later the collectives became collectives of a more advanced form and finally a part of the Communes in 1958. Under the Commune system, farming was done collectively, with a team of farmers working as a group. Each received work points for their work, according to the number of days they worked. After the team delivered a required amount of output to the government procurement agency, it distributed the rest to the team members according to the work points accrued. Under such a system, the hard work of one team member could lead to an increase in team output but the output would be divided among all team members. Thus individual farmers could not derive much benefit from hard work and had little incentive to produce. In the mean time, in 1957, China started the First Five-Year Plan. Central economic planning was adopted and modeled after the planning system of the Soviet Union. The state enterprises were assigned output quotas and provided with approved amounts of inputs to produce them. China' economy became a planned economy.

The planned economy did not function well. The farmers lost economic incentives to work hard under the Commune system of collective farming. State-owned enterprises were not provided with profit incentives to operate efficiently. The commercial banking system was abolished. The People's Bank and its branch banks accepted deposits from the Chinese citizens but did not extend loans on the basis of the credit worthiness of the borrowers. These banks had to extend loans to state-owned enterprises as directed by the central planning authorities that approved the loans. China's economy was operating inefficiently, as the economic reformers in the late 1970s recognized.

Two Disastrous Political Movements

Besides the shortcomings of the system of central economic planning, the Chinese population suffered a great deal from two political movements initiated and orchestrated by the Communist Party Chairman Mao Zedong. The first was the Great Leap

Forward Movement of 1958. Mao converted the farm collectives into Communes in only a few months from April to September 1958. The Great Leap was launched by Mao to enable China to catch up very rapidly with the more advanced countries in one great leap. Unreasonably high production targets were assigned. To increase the output of steel, the people used furnaces in their backyards to convert finished steel products back to raw steel to satisfy the large output quota for steel. Under the Commune system, collective farming affected adversely efficiency in production while collective dining in mass dining halls generated waste in consumption. Economic incentive was destroyed and agriculture output was greatly reduced. What was produced was wasted when people ate together in mass dining halls, as compared with eating separately as farm families. The greatest famine in Chinese history occurred in the early 1960s with over 20 million lives lost as a result. The government attributed the famine to bad weather conditions.

For those readers interested in estimating the number of lives lost from the Great Leap, the following arithmetical exercise may be revealing. According to government official statistics published in *Statistical Yearbook of China* by the Chinese State Statistics Bureau, from 1958 to 1961, the birth rates per thousand persons in the population were 29.22, 24.78, 20.86 and 18.02, and the death rates were 11.98, 14.59, 25.43 and 14.24 respectively. The more normal birth rate in 1957 was 34.03 and the death rate was 10.80. Hence the deficit birth rates per thousand persons from 1958 to 1961 were 4.81, 9.25, 13.17, 16.01 and the extra death rates were 1.18, 3.79, 14.63, and 3.44 respectively. Multiplying the extra death rates by the corresponding population figures of 0.660, 0.672, 0.662, and 0.658 billion and summing the products for the four years give 15.274 million extra deaths in the four years attributable to the failure of the Great Leap. In addition, if we allow for most of the deficit births as resulting from miscarriages and failures to conceive due to malnutrition of the mothers, we could come up with estimates of the total loss of the Chinese population in the order of 27 million persons. The economic harm of the Great Leap was enormous.

The second movement was the Cultural Revolution. It was started by Mao after he had lost his political power as a result of the failure of the Great Leap. More moderate leaders of the Communist Party assumed power in the early 1960s. To regain political power Mao appealed directly to the Chinese youth at the expense of the Party and government establishment which he had created and led for two decades. He exhorted the youths and the teenagers to become Red Guards and through a Cultural Revolution to remove the remnants of a decadent culture that included Confucianism and capitalism. Old books and art treasures were destroyed in museums and homes. People accused of living by the old cultural tradition or practicing the capitalist way of life were paraded on the streets. Children participated in such activities against their parents, and students against their professors or teachers. Any person having a relative living in a capitalist country could be a suspect. Many intellectuals died. China was in chaos during this period from 1966 to 1976. Any person could be accused of being a "rightist" and suffered the consequences accordingly. One group of the Red Guards could claim to be the true followers of Mao in fighting against another group who pursued a different course. To show their loyalty to Mao, the young Red Guards were asked to raise a red book containing quotations from the Chairman, and to recite the sayings therein. Economic planning was disrupted. Universities were closed. Urban intellectuals and residents were sent to the countryside to live with and learn from the peasants. It was perhaps the darkest period of China's history. Yet foreign journalists and visitors were shown the best of China artificially staged for their visits in the early 1970s. Many were deceived and reported that China was a utopia.

During the Cultural Revolution, Mao had already decided to open a dialogue with the United States. He welcomed the visit of

President Richard Nixon in 1972. Mao passed away in September 1976. His four followers who had led the Cultural Revolution, called the Gang of Four, were arrested, put to trial and convicted. The more pragmatic leaders of the Party assumed control.

Economic Reform Initiated in 1978

The Cultural Revolution made the Chinese Communist Party very unpopular. Many moderate members of the Party including Deng Xiaoping also suffered during the Cultural Revolution. When Deng succeeded as the leader of the Party in 1978, he initiated economic reforms in the 11th Party Congress. This was to be a 180-degree turn from the previous economic system that practiced central planning. A major reform was needed to dissociate the new leadership from the previous one responsible for the Cultural Revolution. The reform took place also because the more enlightened Party members and government officials had learned the shortcomings of central planning. In the meantime they witnessed the economic success of neighboring economies, including those of Hong Kong, Singapore, Taiwan and South Korea, called the Four Little Dragons. The first three were the accomplishments of fellow Chinese. The contrasting economic performance of South and North Korea, and of West and East Germany reinforced the belief that central planning did not work well. The reform towards a market-oriented economy also had the support of the Chinese people who disliked the system as they had suffered through the planning period with the shortage of consumer goods.

Collective farming was soon abandoned in favor of private farming. Each farm family was assigned a piece of land so that they could farm for their own benefits, after they were required to deliver a fixed quota of their output to the team leader. The team leader could use these outputs to satisfy the quota of total output that he needed to deliver to the government procurement agency.

Previously, the team leader directed the farmers in his team to farm as a group on a large piece of land. As a result of this change, farm output increased dramatically in 1979 and the early 1980s. This success served as the foundation for other reforms.

To reform the urban economy, production and distribution under the direction of central planning were changed step by step. State enterprises were first given some autonomy in their output decisions. After paying taxes to the government they could retain the remainder of their profits for their own use, whereas previously all of their revenues were treated as government revenues. The forces of market supply and demand, beginning in the middle 1980s, were gradually allowed to set commodity prices. A dual price system was in operation. Under this system, the government-regulated prices remained in force for specified quantities of inputs used by state-owned enterprises and specified quantities of the outputs that they produced. At the same time additional amounts of these inputs and outputs were allowed to be sold at (usually higher) prices determined by market forces. A state enterprise being allocated given amounts of inputs at regulated prices could go to the market to purchase more inputs at market prices. It had to sell a certain amount of its output at the lower regulated price but could sell the remaining output at a higher market price. Elementary economics tells us that the lower cost for acquiring the given amounts of inputs at regulated prices is equivalent to a fixed subsidy, and the lower revenue due to selling a given amount of output at a lower price is equivalent to a fixed tax. Neither affects the economic calculations of the enterprise that would lead to an efficient operation, because the calculations are based on the market prices of the extra inputs required and of the extra output to be sold. Hence the dual price system was an effective system in the allocation of resources before all prices were set by market forces.

Besides relaxing control over state-owned enterprises, the government allowed and even encouraged the establishment of private and collective enterprises. The slogans condemning the evil of capitalism were changed to "getting rich is glorious." Township and village enterprises, established by local governments that had economic resources and political standing, behaved like private enterprises in a western capitalist economy with similar economic incentives. They were the most dynamic sector of the economy, surpassing the state-owned enterprises in total output in the 1990s. Most important of all, the open door policy was a drastic change, opening China's door to foreign trade and investment. Foreign investment provided China with capital, managerial skill and modern technology, as well as competition for domestic enterprises to improve their performance. Much of foreign investment came from Hong Kong, Taiwan, and overseas Chinese in other parts of the world. The rapid growth and development of China's economy in the two decades (1978–1998) after economic reform was phenomenal. On average the rate of growth of total output was at a rate of 9.6 percent per year according to official statistics, and the remarkable growth was for foreign visitors to see.

What accounted for the success of China's economic reform? The government deserved credit in guiding the reform in a gradual process. The process was gradual because government economic officials did not know a particular system to follow. They needed to learn step by step through experimentation. As Deng wisely advised, "Seek truth from facts." This means, in terms of economic reform, "find a right system by observing the results." The gradual process through experimentation was necessary in order to convince the Party members and government officials who had been indoctrinated previously with an orthodox Communist ideology for years to change their thinking and support the new policies. The government maintained the existing political and administrative structure to provide stability in carrying out economic reform. (Political stability was maintained with one interruption by student demonstration in Tiananmen Square. The demonstration began in April 1989 in the form of mourning the death of Communist Party Secretary Hu Yaobang while protesting against government corruption and serious inflation and urging rapid change towards a more democratic government. The demonstration ended in the tragic Tiananmen Square Incident of June 4, 1989.) Once market institutions were established, economic incentives began to operate under the market system. However imperfect, the market institutions provided opportunities for the Chinese to make money by hard work and ingenuity.

Once sufficient opportunities under a set of market institutions are available, the second most important factor contributing to China's economic success is the quality of the Chinese human capital. Like other talented people in the world, the Chinese owe their talents to their social and cultural history. They seem to perform very well in other parts of South-East Asia even when the rules were stacked against them. They have demonstrated their talents in Hong Kong, Singapore and Taiwan. The Chinese workers have good working habits and skills and the Chinese entrepreneurs are resourceful and striving. These traits are inherited from their historical and cultural heritage, which is the main subject of this chapter.

People wonder why China has done so well in the last two and a half decades after the economic reforms started in 1978. From the viewpoint of economic development, China's record is not a miracle. Given political stability and law and order, the three major factors contributing to economic development that China possesses are market economic institutions, high-quality human capital and the advantage of a latecomer in employing the modern technology invented by the first-developed countries, as I will further elaborate in Chapter 3. China should naturally do well as compared with other economies lacking in any of these three important factors. From a historical perspective, China was doing well for a long time. It took a sick leave and has resumed its former path. It has recovered because of its historical heritage that is resilient and because its problem was temporary, only a disorder for one hundred some years in the course of over 4,000 years.

Culture and Daily Life

The cultural heritage of the Chinese refers not only to the treasures in their homes and museums, and the historical sites they visit, but also the enjoyment they derive from good cooking and from the appreciation or practice of calligraphy, painting, martial arts, literature, and important philosophical ideas. In addition, it includes the skills, good working habits, and business sense that they have learned from their parents, members of their communities, and indirectly from their parents' parents. They use these skills to derive economic benefits, as we will discuss in Chapter 3.

The Chinese live well because of what they have inherited from an old and long-living civilization. Unlike other great ancient civilizations in Mesopotamia, Egypt and Greece thousands of years ago, the Chinese culture has survived and evolved. Much has been accumulated from the past for the benefit of the present generation and people around the world. Most of the activities that the Chinese enjoy as a part of this long-living culture are not included in the calculation of national income. Economists treat some of these activities as productive activities at home or as consumption (leisure) activities but do not regard them as a part of productive activities included in national income accounting. If a Chinese cooks good food at home for the consumption of his family members, every one in the family leads a good life that is not measured by national income statistics. Some of these leisure activities are discussed in this chapter, but the discussion is by no means comprehensive. This discussion supplements Chapter 3 on economic output to describe the quality of life in China.

Food and Cooking

Chinese food is considered to be among the best in the world. How good a certain kind of food is depends partly on a person's taste. Taste is in turn influenced and cultivated by past habits. The Chinese have paid a lot of attention to food. They spend much time preparing it, enjoying it and talking about it. Others who have learned to appreciate Chinese food do the same.

Having learned from many past generations, the Chinese have acquired good culinary skills. They enjoy the result at home every day. Chinese cooking can be simple or complicated. Some dishes can take a long time to prepare while others take only a minute or two. A dish of vegetables stir-fried in the wok can be ready in less than one minute. It tastes good if the wok has the right temperature, the timing is perfect and the cook has given it the right touch. Temperature, timing and ingredients can be recorded in a cookbook but the result depends on the skill of the chef. While any one can follow a cookbook, it requires a great chef to produce a great dish. The price of a dish served in a good restaurant, which presumably reflects its quality, is determined to a large extent by the quality of the cook. Most Chinese who cook at home are good cooks. Some years ago, cooks in Chinese restaurants in the United States were seldom professional cooks in China, for the latter earned a good living before 1949, and did not see the need to emigrate. The emigrants were mostly people who could not make a decent living in China. Yet some became cooks in the United States simply because they had the basic culinary skills that the Chinese had. Their home-cooking skills were good enough to make their way to a Chinese restaurant to make money.

Cooking is an art. Good cooks are artists that use their instinct and intuition. People living in traditional China did not use cookbooks. They learned by receiving instructions from and observing their teachers, and by memory and practice. When the skill is acquired, it is displayed naturally and by instinct. As the Chinese do not use cookbooks, they seldom measure the ingredients. Yet they know exactly how much salt or oil to add when they stir-fry a vegetable or prepare a meat dish. This may be likened to an oil painter who does not measure the amount of each kind of paint when he paints. This yields a different result each time, but they are all of good quality if the artist is good. Quality of life in China is so much better because people know how to cook good food at home. GNP (Gross National Product) cannot adequately measure the economic wealth of the Chinese. Only the value of vegetables and meat that the Chinese buy is included in GNP, not the value of the home cooked meals consumed, which can be worth many times the cost of the ingredients.

There are regional differences in Chinese food and cooking. Wheat and rice are the staple in the north and the south respectively. Northern Chinese make good dumplings. Shanghainese like meat cooked with plenty of soy sauce and some sugar. People in Guangdong Province in the South prefer lighter dishes. Cooking of fish is rightly timed to prevent overcooking and to preserve the tenderness of the meat. People in Sichuan Province in the West, on the other hand, eat spicy food, some too hot for people from other regions that are not accustomed to it. Many Chinese consider Cantonese food to be the best. Perhaps the Cantonese culinary art is more sophisticated. For example, a Cantonese cook can manipulate the wok rapidly up and down and in different inclinations to control the temperature and to mix the ingredients at the same time. In general, Chinese food is healthy. Both the ingredients and the way of cooking produce healthy food. The Chinese do not have serious diet problems.

Calligraphy and Painting

Calligraphy and painting are two closely related forms of Chinese art. The Chinese invented writing as symbols to represent real objects. These symbols or characters were recorded on turtle shells for fortune telling. Since both writing and painting are pictorial representations, they require similar skills. Being skillful in one makes it easier to acquire skills in the other. After brush and ink were invented, the Chinese have used them for writing. Learning to read and write is the basics of education in China, as in elsewhere. One difference is that the Chinese pay a lot of attention to the quality of a person's handwriting. If it is good, he commands the respect of others. Poor handwriting could cause a person to miss a job opportunity. A good friend once asked me to write down on a piece of paper two dishes that he would like to order. When the waiter saw the order, he was surprised and asked whether my friend had written it. The waiter could not believe that someone learning Chinese in the United States could produce handwriting like that of someone educated in China. An ordinary person serving in a Chinese restaurant could tell the quality of handwriting because calligraphy is so much a part of Chinese culture. Chinese children at the time when I grew up in the 1930s had to practice writing Chinese characters using a brush in school and at home almost every day. Such practice is not as common in China today. As long as a student can write legibly with a pen, it is the content that matters in schools.

Even today many Chinese practice calligraphy. Practicing calligraphy is a satisfying and enriching experience. One gets satisfaction in seeing his writing improve. There is no limit to the level that a person can attain, as in the case of painting or playing a musical instrument. Practice also calms and relaxes a person. It gives her peace of mind, as from meditation. In meditation, a person concentrates on thinking about something beautiful or peaceful. Similarly in practicing calligraphy, one can copy a masterpiece or compose one's own passage that is beautiful and peaceful. Beauty can come from the content of the material that one copies, or from the art of the calligraphy itself. One is not frustrated if the result is bad or the improvement is slow. If one is not satisfied with what he writes, he can easily try again. Failures can be frustrating if there is something to lose. When one writes poorly, nothing is lost except some ink and paper.

In Chinese calligraphy, a well-written character is an elegant composition formed by the different strokes. A well-written passage requires a beautiful composition of the characters. Traditionally, the characters of a passage flow vertically from the top to the bottom, and the columns go from right to left. In a good composition, the vertical lines are straight with one character placed below another. The size of the characters is uniform. The parts of each character of equal importance should be of equal size and well balanced. The lines are parallel and adjacent lines are of the same distance apart. However, these rules should not be followed too strictly. A strict adherence to these rules yields a piece of calligraphy that is dull and not lively. A suitable amount of variation in these rules will yield a more attractive product.

As a beginner, a child starts with copying some standard characters properly written. He learns the composition and the meaning of each character, thereby improving his reading skill as well. Sometimes he would start his lessons by tracing a series of characters printed on the paper. As time progresses, he would copy the calligraphy of the great masters preserved through rubbings. The rubbings were produced by putting ink on a piece of stone carved with the characters written by a master and getting an imprint on a piece of paper. Copying teaches the student discipline. In China discipline comes first before one can create one's own style.

Skill at calligraphy carries over to painting. The two art forms are intertwined in China. Writing was started by drawing images of objects. As writing became an important part of Chinese culture and was used particularly to record events and to communicate with others, the art of calligraphy evolved and improved. The same brush was used to paint. The same skill and hand movements were applied to painting, to the enrichment of both. A stroke that makes a Chinese character beautiful and lively can do the same for the tail of a horse or a bamboo leaf in a painting. In the same session, a Chinese can practice calligraphy and paint. On the same piece of paper, a Chinese can paint and write, resulting in a single composition. The two components complement and enhance each other, in both content and form. In content, a scene of a scholar admiring the moon can be enriched by a poem or part of a poem. In form, the combination — particularly the matching or contrasting styles of individual strokes making up the objects painted and the characters written — makes beautiful compositions. In the same way that the practice of calligraphy improves a person's state of mind, so does painting. Different emotions can be expressed in paintings. Anger is expressed by the painting of bamboo. Bamboo leaves are painted by the movement of one's arms as in wielding a sword. Both the arm movement and the sight of the resulting bamboo branches and leaves help a person express his anger, providing a sense of relief. Other sentiments can be expressed in paintings as well.

To some extent, every Chinese who knows how to write with a brush can appreciate Chinese paintings in terms of the strokes and of the entire composition. If you have practiced the strokes in calligraphy or in painting, you can often appreciate the strokes produced by others. Discipline comes first. An American child is encouraged to draw freely and to put down on a piece of paper anything that comes to mind using his imagination. By contrast, a Chinese child learns discipline before he is being given freedom. He learns to write characters properly before he can deviate from the work of the masters and show his own style and creativity. One does not start to create without first learning the basics. A young American student may learn some basics in painting but is allowed to be creative even before learning the basics. On the other hand, an older American graduate student who wants to be creative in writing his PhD thesis has to learn the fundamentals of his discipline. Both systems may have their merits under different social environments.

Since all educated Chinese practice calligraphy to some extent, they appreciate paintings. The same brush can be used, and similar strokes can be applied to both. Both forms of art are practiced with the arm and sometimes body movements, along with the associated mental state and emotions. As pointed out in Fong (1992, pp. 4–5) appreciation of both takes the form of projecting oneself onto the role of the artist, imagining how he would have produced the object. It is an active participation, taking the role of the calligrapher or the painter in creating the product, and not just viewing the product itself. Good life is enjoyed not only by practicing calligraphy and painting, but also by appreciating the works of others as one projects oneself onto the role of the artist.

Handicraft, Furniture, China, and Other Forms of Art

The Chinese are skillful in making things with their hands. It gives them pleasure to do so, just as in producing good calligraphy and painting. Educated Chinese enjoy carving a seal for himself or for a friend. Chinese seal is used in lieu of a signature to authenticate a piece of document. It requires artistic talent to carve a set of Chinese characters in their mirror image on the flat surface of a piece of stone. The artistic skills can also be observed in Chinese handicraft. The products are available in stores in Hong Kong and other cities in China. They are also available in stores outside China but are perhaps more limited in variety. In the Chinese stores, one can also find Chinese furniture, china sets, cloisonné vases and other age honored quality handicraft. Ming furniture is well known in the world, as are Ming vases. Old Chinese vases are very valuable regardless of the dynasty of origin.

Many museums around the world house China's artistic treasures, but the best is probably the Palace Museum in Taipei, Taiwan. As the name indicates, the treasures therein used to be housed in the Imperial Palace in Beijing during the Qing dynasty. It was then an accumulation of the possessions of the emperors over hundreds of years. When a dynasty was founded, the new emperor took over the rule as well as the possessions of the deposed emperor. The holdings became national treasures under the stewardship of the government of the Republic of China after its establishment in 1911. The government founded a Palace Museum in the premises of the Qing Imperial Palace to exhibit the objects. In 1949 the ROC government took the best pieces to Taipei when it moved to Taiwan, and created a new Palace Museum. The Palace Museum in Taipei is an excellent museum because generations of emperors were the ones responsible for the collection of the most exquisite objects in a country that was full of artistic treasures.

Architecture — Buildings and Gardens

Temples in Kyoto, Japan, represent some of the best Chinese architecture of the Tang period. The Japanese absorbed much Chinese culture during the Tang dynasty. They learned and adopted the Chinese written language, painted Chinese paintings and built their buildings in Chinese style. It is difficult to find ancient Chinese architecture in China because wars and invasions destroyed most of the buildings. The style is simple in form. The early architectural style of Frank Lloyd Wright was influenced by it, before the famous architect went on to create his own.

A distinguishing characteristic of Chinese architecture is that pieces of woods are joined not by nails but by fitting together the properly carved matching connections so as to provide strength to the binding and to the building. The same applies to Chinese furniture. Freestanding columns and mobile partitions in a room or a hall are characteristic of the Chinese architecture that modern Western architecture has adopted. So is the use of panels in a contemporary house. Chinese architecture can be colorful. A building with red brick walls and green tiles on the roof shows the contrast of colors. Such buildings were not uncommon at the time I grew up in the 1930s in Guangzhou (used to be called Canton). My family had such a house, and the university that I later attended had many such buildings. A visitor of Guangzhou today can still spot these buildings in Zhongshan University. Architecture of grand scale is found in the Great Wall and in the Imperial Palace in Beijing, among many other places in China. Contemporary architecture in China is progressing rapidly because of the creativity of the Chinese architects. They have experimented with a variety of forms as can be seen in the contemporary buildings in major cities, especially Shanghai.

Chinese gardens are famous, especially those in the city of Suzhou near Shanghai. There are "hills" made of rocks of all shapes. Children can play hide and seek around them. There are beautiful flowers, as in gardens in other parts of the world. Sometimes ponds are built to add variation. Water, with or without fish, is always attractive and pleasing to people. One segment of a Suzhou styled garden including some surrounding structures can be found at the Metropolitan Museum of Art in New York City. Readers interested in Chinese Gardens may consult Valder (2002).

Martial Arts and Performing Arts

Martial arts have long served as a form of exercise. There are two main forms or schools. One is hard and the other is soft. *Kungfu* as generally known is hard. It is seen in movies, where people use *kungfu* to fight. Any part of the body can be used. Unlike boxing, which does not allow kicking, *kungfu* involves arms and legs, fingers and forehead. There is no rule against the use of any part of the body or against any motion to defend yourself, or to attack your opponents. The strength is shown in the motion and facial expression of the practitioner. The movement is usually fast. It is strenuous to practice *kungfu*. The second form of martial arts is represented by *taichi*. It is composed of slow movements. The movements appear soft, accompanied by the calm facial expression of the practitioner. I am more familiar with *taichi* and will describe it in greater detail.

Taichi consists of one hundred and twelve movements to be performed sequentially, one after another. Each movement has to be precisely executed. The motion is slow. It takes at least half an hour to complete the sequence of movements if one performs them properly. Each movement has a name. Some sequences of movements are repeated. Each movement can be applied to defend oneself or to attack the opponent as needed. During practice, the person contemplates the presence of an opponent and imagines applying each movement in a two-person contest. Although one does not use an apparent force, there is strength hidden in each movement as one imagines defending himself or attacking an opponent. Body weight is shifted from one leg to the other in each movement, while the legs are seldom straight, except in several kicking motions with one leg extended. The shifting of body weight from one leg to the other helps blood circulation and strengthens one's legs. The idea is to develop strength by the mental control of each part of the body, and not by use of brute force. *Taichi* masters often win when facing opponents using a hard form of *kungfu*. An ordinary person practicing *taichi* as daily exercise may not know how to fight, unless he wants to take additional lessons for actual fighting. He benefits from it not only as a physical exercise but also as a mental exercise for relaxation and concentration in thinking about the movements. Concentration is required to follow the entire sequence of movements because some sections are similar and can lead to confusion. Lack of concentration is discovered if a wrong sequence is performed and it should be corrected. The beautiful movements are like a dance. I have seen a *taichi* master over 80 years of age walking like a teenager. Her body is balanced and steady. Her steps are light, requiring no effort. All this comes from daily practice of *taichi*.

Also requiring disciplined body movements are certain forms of performing arts. One form beloved by the Chinese is opera. Each region of China has its own form of opera. In the eyes of a novice, operas in different regions are similar and might be called Peking opera, but they are different to an expert. This art form is not easy for Westerners to appreciate. They find the singing and the accompanying musical instruments too loud and the voice of the singers shrieking. To the Chinese who can understand, the voice of each type of singers is appreciated, as it expresses the appropriate role of a female or a male singer. Often a female in an opera is performed by a man, and vice versa. Besides the voice, the body movement is extremely important. Good performers move all parts of the body gracefully, harmonized by corresponding facial expressions to express some act or feeling. The stage is simply propped with a table and one or two chairs. Stylistic miming is needed to indicate the opening of a door when there is no door on the stage or the riding of a horse when there is no horse. Joy and sorrow under different circumstances are expressed by both facial and body movements, and by various hand gestures. Such acting, if one can call it so, is a highly sophisticated art form. One enjoys opera singing not only by watching and listening to the performance of others, but also by performing it oneself at home. A group of friends would get together to sing and act out the scenes as people do in *karaoke*.

Performing arts also take the form of acrobatics performed on stage. Some forms of acrobatics are performed as part of an opera if the story calls for such. A variety show can be made up of acrobatics, singing, dancing, and magic shows. Foreign visitors enjoy such shows and they admire the talents of the performers. The Chinese performers are very good. Young people often learn acrobatics and *kungfu* at the same time because the skills are similar. Children start acrobatic training at a very young age when their body is flexible to accommodate difficult movements. The best stage shows in Las Vegas and other places requiring agility at dangerously high places employ many performers originally trained in China.

I have not discussed Chinese music except as a part of Peking opera where both instruments and voice are appreciated. Chinese music in ancient times was imported from the Middle East, or was at least influenced by Middle Eastern music. One reads in Tang poetry about beautiful dances accompanied by music, including the long poem glorifying the love affair between the Tang emperor and his concubine mentioned in Chapter 1. Since music was performed by memory and not recorded, the scores were lost. Recent research has attempted to recover some ancient scores and to find out how ancient music sounded. Musical instruments have survived. String instruments and drums feature importantly in Peking operas. Ordinary Chinese plays wind instruments. Gongs featured importantly in the symphony performed in the evening of June 30, 1997 to celebrate the return of Hong Kong to China the following day.

Chinese Medicine and Ways of Healing

Through thousands of years, the Chinese have discovered effective medicine and ways of healing. Chinese medicine may not be fully appreciated by those who are familiar with Western medicine. In recent years, it has become better appreciated. Chinese medicine is effective because it is based on knowledge accumulated over a long period of time while Western medicine has a much shorter history. Chinese medicine was not discovered by scientific method, but scientific method is not the only way to discover useful knowledge. Even if the scientific method is a systematic and efficient way to find good medicine, less efficient methods applied to collect information for a much longer period of time can produce results as good as or even better than Western medicine for the treatment of certain illnesses.

There are a number of illnesses that can be better treated by Chinese medicine simply because the Chinese have spent many more years searching for and trying out different herbs to treat different illnesses. For example, kidney stones can pass through the urine track by taking Chinese herbal medicine without an operation. There are numerous other examples of effective Chinese medicine and ways of healing, as the Chinese have depended on them for centuries. A number of Western medical researchers have discovered the effectiveness of certain kinds of Chinese medicine and have tried to perform chemical analyses to find out how to produce them. Chinese acupuncture is now fairly widely accepted and practiced in the United States.

Many educated Chinese still use Chinese medicine in addition to Western medicine. I once visited the hospital associated with Peking University for the treatment of certain illness, and the doctor asked me whether I would like to take Chinese or Western medicine. I thought for a while and chose Chinese medicine because I thought it was effective for the illness, although I believed that Western medicine would work too. For the treatment of SARS (severe acute respiratory syndrome) in the Spring of 2003, the Chinese medical profession applied both Chinese and Western medicine to the patients. Both the experts and the general public in China believed that Chinese medicine was helpful in this case. One basic function of Chinese herbal medicine is believed to be to help strengthen the resistance of the body against diseases, as a healthy person is more likely to recover from illness.

Literature

Chinese literature began with the invention of writing thousands of years ago. During the Zhou dynasty over 3,000 years ago, China had advanced forms of essays, poetry and history. Good historical records, such as the *Book of Spring and Autumn* that depicts the events of that period, is also good literature. *Records of the Historian* written by Sima Qian of the Han dynasty over 2,000 years ago, with a passage quoted in Chapter 1, is also considered good literature.

A high point of Chinese literature appeared during the Qing dynasty in the novel *The Dream of Red Chambers* by the scholar-novelist Cao Xueqin. It is an impressive novel in many respects. Ordinary Chinese read it repeatedly for its contents and literary style. Scholars consider this book by itself as a field of study just as economics or mathematics. Some spend their lifetime studying this one novel. A course devoted to the study of this novel is offered in some American universities although it may cover only selected parts of its contents. If one wonders why the contents of this book can standalone as a field of study, one can think of it as representing a multidisciplinary subject. Modern scholarship tends to be specialized and fragmented into fields. Pre-modern scholars, like Benjamin Franklin, were good in many areas now classified as fields. In this novel one finds prose, poetry, human psychology, sociology and architecture, among other subjects.

The novel is about a large family connected with the imperial government as one member once served the emperor. One of his daughters was the emperor's concubine. The main character was a young man having close relations with a number of young women; some were his cousins and some his attendants. There are 120 chapters, each fascinating and possibly devoted to one topic such as poetry or architecture. There are hundreds of poems. The poems attributed to each person have their distinguished characteristics reflecting the talents and personality of the assumed author. The subjects of the poems are extensive. One chapter is devoted to architecture, with descriptions of different architectural styles. Another one is devoted to opera, and so forth. Knowledge of such a large number of subjects is woven into the stories about a large number of people. Descriptions of action, emotion and human relations are lively and penetrating. The end of each chapter gives the reader suspense to wait for the next, as the novel was written and published chapter by chapter. The reader can view the author as a scholar teaching many subjects as he is telling a long story.

I touched upon Tang poetry briefly in Chapter 1. Tang poems are rigid in form, with an equal number of words (either five or seven) per line, and an equal number of lines (usually four) per poem or per section of a poem that has many sections. The last words of the first, second and forth lines should rhyme, while the last word of the third line provides a contrast or a pause for the harmonizing fourth line to come. Reading or reciting poems is like chanting. Emotions aroused by the poem are expressed by reading it out loud. One can enjoy reading a novel silently, but gets much more enjoyment from reading a poem aloud and even with motions of the head and body. A poem can describe nature, humans, and relations among humans or human reactions to nature. A description of nature's reaction to men in a poem can be used to bring out men's understanding and appreciation of nature in their own terms. A poem can also tell an interesting story. As all these are expressed in a specified form and in words that rhyme, one can enjoy them by reciting from memory.

Tang poetry is still read, recited and written by the Chinese people today. Other forms of poetry have been developed. Poetry of the Song dynasty that followed Tang had more variations in one respect and was more rigid in another. It had unequal number of words per line, but people tended to follow exactly the same composition structure of a previously well-known poem. This means that the follower had to use the same number of words in the same line and make the lines rhyme the same way. Instead of writing a Song-style poem, people call it "filling in" a poem. Literally the follower would use the lines of the model poem and fill in the words. The poems of the famous scholar-poet Su Shi are favorite model poems. An admirer-follower put words to "fill in" the words of one well-known poem of his. Centuries after Song, scholars in the Republic of China adopted Western, mainly English or French, style of poetry that allows for more variations in the length of lines and in structure. Educated Chinese not only recite poetry but also write poems for self-enjoyment and to share with their friends.

Philosophy

Chinese philosophy is characterized by its variety and depth. During the period of Spring and Autumn at the end of the Zhou dynasty over 2,000 years ago, many schools of thought flourished. Scholars studying the different philosophies of this and later periods can find in them many of the main philosophical ideas of the present day. Confucius had much to say about ways for self-improvement, ethics, good human relations and social harmony. There is an entire ethical system to guide individual behavior and to achieve social order. Besides Confucianism, Legalism and Naturalism were also parts of the Chinese philosophical tradition. Rather than choosing just one school, an ordinary Chinese would choose the best from different schools, and the most suitable as circumstances require. A person practicing Confucianism in his role as a scholar can take a rest or a step back from his certain personal problems by following Daoism's "to do nothing." Doing nothing means to let nature take its course, or to let things evolve naturally. One may be facing a difficult decision. Agonizing over alternative courses of action can be energy consuming and frustrating. It may be better to follow Daoism and let nature take its own course. Many a time the problem is resolved by itself. Of course, not all problems are resolved by themselves, but one can be wise enough to choose inaction at the right moment. Likewise, a Chinese can follow different religions; he can visit a Buddhist temple and listen to a Daoist monk in the same day. Both religions can be good for the person. Chinese in general do not believe in absolute truth, or the existence of only one god. This attitude can help them to be more tolerant.

The Chinese are realists. Chinese philosophy tends to be more concerned with human affairs as compared to speculations about the supernatural. Purely abstract speculations as in metaphysics are uncommon, although some Daoists can be speculative. Philosophical questions such as how one knows that one exists are not appealing to them. Many do not see the point of asking such questions. They know they exist. Taking one's own existence for granted is such a natural assumption that challenging it can be considered fruitless if not unreasonable. The Chinese are pragmatic as they devote their energy in solving the problems of living. For example, when asked about god or the spirits Confucius said, "let us talk about humans first" or "I do not discuss god or the spirits." A trove of moral and political philosophy exists in Chinese history.

There are many books to read, covering topics in economics, law and sociology before these topics were divided into different fields. Readers interested in Chinese philosophy may consult Chan (1963).

Confucian Philosophy and Daily Life

As mentioned earlier, one branch of Chinese philosophy that has had most impact on the daily life of the Chinese is Confucian philosophy. Here, I would like to discuss its social impact as a philosophical system.

Individual Conduct

Confucius' teaching is recorded in three major books that many children of my generation read and all children of my father's generation read. One is on "Great Learning," one on "the Golden Mean," and one on his "Dialogues" as recorded by his disciples. This may be likened to the teaching of Jesus Christ. He had never written any book but his disciples recorded his sayings. The basic ideas on living a good life are based on loyalty, piety, kindness, love, reliability, righteousness, and peaceful living. All are rules governing a person's behavior in order to achieve social harmony. A subject is to be loyal to his master, emperor or country. A child is to practice piety towards the parents. The other words cited above have obvious meanings. As Confucius advises, to achieve self-fulfillment, one should first learn by observing and understanding the world. Then one can be determined and set a right goal in order to discipline oneself, before he can achieve family harmony, or rule the country and eventually help achieve a peaceful world order. Another important Confucian teaching is that in daily living do not take the extremes but select the "Golden Mean."

Family Relationship

From teaching the individual, Confucius teaches how to attain family harmony. Having each member play an assigned role is a solution. The children must obey and respect their parents. The parents should love the children. The wife must follow her husband, but the husband must love and care for his wife. (Needless to say, what Confucius taught in a traditional Chinese cultural setting is not necessarily appropriate in a modern American society.) A younger brother should yield to his older brother. Unlike the situation in a modern American family, age or birth order is important in determining the status of a member, as between older and younger brothers. There is no single Chinese word for "brother" but two different words for "older brother" (兄) and "younger brother" (弟). To express the word "brother" one has to combine these two words (兄弟). The ordering of relation by age applies to friends too. If you were older, a younger friend would yield to you. Such ordering seems strange for American families but was still practiced when I grew up.

Besides placing each member of a family in his/her rightful place, family unity and mutual help are important. Individualism teaches one to care for oneself first, and care for others as much as one pleases. But collectivism in Chinese family means that one should automatically sacrifice oneself for the good of the family. If one person is well to do, all members of the family share the benefits. In my family, my father happened to make more money than his father and all his brothers and sisters. He shared his wealth with all other members, including his cousins and second cousins, and thus their families. When the war with Japan began in 1937, our family moved to a fairly large house in Hong Kong, which my father owned. Then the refugee relatives from Mainland China also moved into our house (including second and third cousins and their families). At one time there were about 65 persons including servants and gardeners living under one roof. The Chinese family system is not only based on Confucian teaching but also has its historical background in the need for people in the same village to protect themselves against attacks from outside. This need has created an extended family system in which membership is extended to all members of the same village. The Chinese regard "being of the same village" as indicating a close tie.

Close family relations sometimes form the basis of family businesses or ordinary businesses in China and in other East-Asian countries rooted in Confucian culture. The head of the family or the business tends to employ family members in the business. Such discrimination has the effect of excluding some possibly more talented persons outside the family from joining the business. Family unity and loyalty have the advantage of providing teamwork which is needed in dealing with crisis situations. Willingness to cooperate and to sacrifice oneself, rather than just protecting one's own interest, can be helpful to the business enterprise.

Social Order

Confucian ethics and moral standard form the basis of a social order. The five basic virtues of a citizen include love (kindness), righteousness, proper social conduct, wisdom and trustworthiness. In addition, mutual respect, honesty and devotion should guide human relations. Social order is built upon the moral conduct of individual members, and not simply by the enforcement of laws under a legal system, as we will further discuss in Chapter 3 on economic behavior. The ruler is advised to guide by kindness and to govern by virtue and respect, and not to lead by edict and administer by punishment. The citizens will thereby follow willingly and conscientiously, and not simply obey without conscience.

The collective good rather than individual rights are emphasized. A market economy achieved by each individual economic agent maximizing his own welfare was functioning in China and well understood by the historian Sima Qian in the Han dynasty.

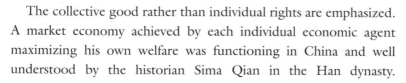

However, in the utopia of Confucius every one is supposed to share what he has. In a well-known passage describing the utopia, the world is said to belong to all people. Individual ownership is not the ideal. Rather, every one in this commonwealth should regard the parents of others as his own, and love the children of others as his own. There is a certain socialist ideal in the sense of all sharing and all contributing to the common good. Although private property has existed in China for a long time, subject to the approval of the emperor, individual members of a society are asked to give and not to take, to endure and not to be aggressive, to be patient and not to be in a hurry, and to reflect on oneself rather than placing the blame on others. Tolerance is more important than freedom.

Concluding Remarks

Chinese culture has lasting value partly because profound philosophical ideas are enduring. These ideas are built on that part of human experience that is little affected by the advancement of science and technology. Modern science and technology change rapidly, but some characteristics of human relations change much more slowly. Good literature, good history and good poetry endure, as do profound philosophical ideas. While old ideas in science and technology need to be replaced by new ones for the sake of progress, Plato and Aristotle are still read by students of philosophy today. Similarly, the heritage of Chinese moral and political philosophy is enduring.

In this chapter, I have tried to illustrate how the quality of life of the Chinese is enhanced by the arts of cooking, calligraphy and painting, handicraft, martial arts and performing arts, knowledge of medicine, literature and poetry, philosophy and the humanistic way of life. These are the result of learning and practicing by a people with a long history.

When a reader sees the title of this chapter, "culture and daily life," she may be thinking of the poverty in China that may prevent many Chinese from having a good quality of life. Many Chinese did not and still do not enjoy some of the cultural treasures mentioned above, but many of the treasures such as good cooking and the practice of *taichi* are available to poor families. Others can be enjoyed as long as one has an opportunity to learn them. Moral codes apply to the rich and the poor. It is important to increase the level of education among the Chinese so that more people can benefit from China's cultural tradition. In discussing the subject "culture and daily life", I have concentrated on what the Chinese culture has to offer, with some benefiting a larger segment of the population than others.

The Economy

The Chinese economy has been growing very rapidly in the last 25 years. It is now essentially capitalistic. China is ruled by the Chinese Communist Party and it did practice central economic planning for 25 years from 1953 to 1978. As an economist interested in China, I have followed the development of the Chinese economy since 1980. Some of my research is reported in Chow (1985, 1994, 2002). Here I will try to answer a few important questions concerning the Chinese economy for the general reader. What was the Chinese economy like before 1949? What is its current condition? How large is it? How fast is it growing and can it be expected to grow rapidly in the next two decades? How much income disparity is there among different regions? What are the strengths and weaknesses of China's economic institutions and their special characteristics?

China's Economy before 1949

Let us begin with the state of the Chinese economy in the 1930s before the Sino-Japanese war started in 1937. It was essentially an agrarian economy with over 85 percent of the population engaged in agriculture. However, industrialization had taken place and financial markets had been developed. In spite of political instability as described in Chapter 1, the Chinese with energy and resourcefulness were able to develop the economy under the existing set of market institutions, while the government was developing the economic infrastructure. The economy in the 1930s was a well-functioning market economy.

The Chinese farmers knew how to farm, as they had learned from generations of farmers preceding them. The number of farmers per acre of farm land was much larger than that in the United States, but the output per acre of land was comparable, as the Chinese used the abundant labor to do the work of farm machinery in the United States. The Chinese knew what crops to plant in a particular location and the method of crop rotation. Much useful information about Chinese agriculture during that period can be found in Buck (1930).

Chinese industry was mainly light industry producing consumer goods like textiles, clothing, paper, toys and matches. It was concentrated in coastal cities, especially in Shanghai. Chinese banks flourished and were functioning like the modern commercial banks of the more developed economies at the time. There was a well-functioning stock market in Shanghai. The government had built railroads, highways, ports, telephone lines and power plants for the generation of electricity in a number of towns and cities. Part of this development was aided by foreign investment. Foreign-owned industrial, commercial and financial enterprises, especially in the leased territories along the coastal areas, served as examples for the development of Chinese enterprises. Certainly even if there had not been such foreign enterprises in China, the Chinese could have learned to set them up themselves, but there is no doubt that the foreign enterprises helped train Chinese managers and workers, introduced modern technology and provided competition for the domestic enterprises. This was a positive aspect of foreign imperialism.

A major lesson to learn from studying the Chinese market economy in the 1930s is that given the opportunities available in a market economy and the technology invented by the developed countries, the Chinese people themselves are capable of developing the economy provided that there is a certain required degree of political stability. The earlier developed economies around the world have followed essentially this route, including the four little dragons or tigers (dragons in Chinese and tigers in English), Hong Kong, Singapore, Taiwan and South Korea. It should not be surprising that once China adopted market institutions after the economic reform in 1978, the economy has grown so rapidly. Market institutions, good-quality human capital and the availability of modern technology are sufficient for rapid economic growth.

The functioning of the Chinese economy was disrupted by the Sino-Japanese war of 1937, the Second World War of 1941–1945 and the civil war between the Nationalists and the Communists until the establishment of the People's Republic of China in 1949. After several years of economic recovery from these wars, China introduced the planning system as we described in Chapter 1. Chapter 1 also described briefly the process of economic reform since 1978 in order to establish a socialist market economy. I will now discuss the present-day Chinese economy in detail.

Chinese Economy at Present

After over two decades of economic reform the Chinese economy at present is essentially a market economy. When you travel to China, you will find that a market economy is functioning, with only a little trace of economic planning. The remnants of the planned economy could be discovered only by a keen observer who looks into the inner working of state-owned enterprises and state-owned commercial banks. As a tourist you will find that consumer goods are plentiful and of good quality. You can get a good hotel and plane or train tickets to travel wherever you wish. You can buy almost anything you wish. You will find that in major cities the Chinese live quite well. They dress well, go to restaurants and theatres, and visit parks and museums. Many have cars. They are tourists in China and elsewhere. They can start and operate businesses to make money, so you can see private shops, department stores, restaurants and private companies. They invest in the Shanghai and Shenzhen Stock Markets, where 1,198 companies are listed with the total value of all stocks traded amounting to about 4.3 trillion *yuan* in 1993. You see no trace of communism in the sense of a tight control of the population as people can move around and speak freely (more on this point in Chapter 6). People are exposed to Western ideas. More and more people can speak English, and some, very well. They read English magazines and books, listen to Western music and watch movies produced in Hollywood. They have friends and relatives studying or working abroad. In Shanghai, intermarriages between Chinese and foreign citizens increased from fewer than 400 in 1980 to 2,705 in 2002. Out of these, 40 percent were with Japanese, 38 percent with people from Hong Kong, Macao or Taiwan and 6.3 percent with people from the United States, as reported in the *People's Daily*, on June 9, 2002. This suggests a convergence in life style among the Chinese and the people from outside.

People living in the countryside near the coastal areas or around some interior cities appear to live well. There are nicely built houses, decked with color TV sets and refrigerators. Many formerly rural areas have been developed into small modern towns with modern apartment houses, nicely-paved roads lined with stores and restaurants, beautiful parks and modern schools and theatres. The Pearl River Delta area in the Southern part of Guangdong province near Hong Kong and the Yangtze River Delta area near Shanghai are especially rich and have been growing rapidly. Manufacturing activities take place in these and other formerly rural areas, making consumer goods including furniture that are exported to the world market. People carry their cell phones and use them frequently while walking. In Suzhou, not far from Shanghai, one sees remnants of the old culture alongside modern technological development. There are high-tech companies mushrooming somewhat like, though not quite up to the standard of, Silicon Valley in California. Although there are poor people in the interior and Western provinces, most people in these areas have enough to eat and look healthy. I will discuss the problem of regional disparity later in this chapter.

Behind this dynamic economy, there is also inefficiency and corruption, both associated with the Chinese bureaucratic system. Foreign and domestic investors have to deal with bureaucrats to establish a new business, or to maintain the smooth operation of an existing business. The bureaucrats in the government have the authority to issue permits and to grant permission for a business to operate. The bureaucrats in state-owned enterprises and state-owned commercial banks have power of control over scarce resource that an investor may need in running his business. The bureaucrats often extract compensation for the services they perform. Corruption in various degrees is widespread, as will be discussed in Chapter 6. Officially the Chinese government calls the Chinese economy a "socialist market economy." A more apt term would be "a bureaucratic market economy."

Size of the Economy

How large is the total output of the Chinese economy? Before discussing total output, let me first acknowledge that the use of economic output as a measure of economic welfare has its limitations. Quality of life that is affected by leisure activities at home as discussed in the last chapter is not measured by economic output. Even in terms of economic output itself, scholars have in recent years pointed out that the degradation of the environment as a result of production should be included in the measurement of economic welfare. In addition, the measurement of economic welfare is subjective to some extent. Consider the economic welfare for people living in rural China in the 19th century who hated the sight of railroads. From their point of view, the construction of railroads reduced their welfare. The railroads disturbed the mountain gods, they thought. This is one aspect of the degradation of the environment, unless the people consider the sight of a railroad attractive.

A modern economist favoring free trade may find it difficult to understand why the Chinese and the Japanese did not want to open their doors to trade with foreigners. Western traders had to force their way into China and Japan. Comprador Perry opened the door of Japan in 1861. After the Opium War of 1840, the British forced China to open its door for trade. The Chinese and the Japanese felt that they were living happily without the foreigners coming to trade with them. Today some Europeans do not like certain American imports such as soft drinks, fast food and pop music as these products were considered undesirable for the society. Other Europeans choose to consume these products. Before the Opium War, some Chinese chose to smoke opium imported by the British. All goods produced are included in national income even if some might have undesirable effects on health. We should be mindful of the above qualifications when we try to measure economic welfare purely in terms of the consumption of economic output in the course of economic globalization.

How can we compare the total output of one country with that of another? If there is only one product, such as steel, the answer is simply obtained by comparing the outputs of steel in the two countries. In fact total output in each country consists of different products. There are apples and oranges, steel and potatoes. Total output for one country is measured by the total market value of all goods and services produced to get a national output figure in current prices of that country. We can do the same for a second country. The first country may have prices expressed in dollars, and the second country, in *yuan*. One can compare the total outputs of the two countries by using the prices (say in dollars) of the first country to evaluate the output of the second country. The total outputs of the two countries both measured in dollars can then be compared. Alternatively, one can use the prices (say in *yuan*) of the second country to evaluate the outputs of both countries and compare them as measured in *yuan*. These two methods yield different answers, as one can expect. In fact the World Bank has performed such an exercise to compare the total outputs of the

United States and China, using the dollar prices to evaluate the Chinese outputs. According to the calculation of the World Bank in its report *Entering the 21st Century* (2000; Table 1, p. 230) the total output in China in 1998 was half of that of the United States, if valued at the dollar prices of the United States. The Chinese total output in 1998 amounts to US$3983.6 billion.

Using this World Bank estimate of China's output in 1998 as the starting point, we can project the outputs of China and the United States to the year 2020. Beginning with the fact that total output in China in 1998 was half that of the United States, let us assume that China's total output will grow at a conservative rate of 6 percent per year on average from 1998 onward for 22 years. From 1998 to 2002, China's growth rate was between 7.5 to 8.0 percent. From 1978 to 1998, it was 9.6 percent. If the Chinese economy were to grow at a modest six percent on average for 22 years from 1998 to 2020, it would require the US economy to grow at 2.9 percent per year on average during this period to produce as much total output as that of the Chinese economy by 2020. Since a 6 percent growth is a conservative estimate for China and a 2.9 percent growth is perhaps a reasonable forecast for the United States, one can conclude that by the year 2020 or its whereabouts, China's economy will be as large as that of the US in terms of total output.

Is this optimistic projection of the size of the Chinese economy reasonable? First, can we rely on the Chinese official statistics to estimate the past growth rates of the economy? Second, can we project substantial growth of the past into the future? Let us examine these two questions one by one.

Accuracy of Chinese Official Statistics

Some skeptics have questioned the accuracy of Chinese official statistics, on which our discussion is based. I believe that the official statistics are by and large accurate enough for the purposes that I have used them. First, for the purpose of studying long-term trends, we can tolerate sizable inaccuracies on the levels of the variables. For example, if Chinese GDP is overestimated by the Chinese State Statistical Bureau by 20 percent, and our purpose is to study the rate of growth of GDP (Gross Domestic Product) from 1978 to 2000. Such overestimation of the GDP will not affect our estimate of the rate of growth if the overestimation occurs fairly consistently. Even if the overestimation is not proportional, say by 10 percent in 1978 and by 20 percent in 1998, the average rate of growth estimated by comparing the levels of GDP in these two years will not be affected substantially. This point is a matter of arithmetic. To illustrate, according to official data, China's GDP (measured in constant 1978 *yuan*) was 362.4 billion in 1978 and 2312.9 billion in 1998. The exponential rate of growth in this 20-year period is $[\ln(2312.9) - \ln(362.4)]/20$ or 0.09268, corresponding to an annual rate of growth of $\exp(0.09268) = 1.096$ or 9.6 percent per year. A skeptic can challenge the estimate 362.4 for GDP in 1978 or the estimate 2312.9 for GDP in 1998 if he can provide sufficient supporting arguments and documentation. Let both the 1978 and the 1998 GDP be overestimates, but the latter be an overestimate by as much as 30 percent more, relative to the former. We therefore should revise it downward from 2312.9 billion to 1779.2 billion *yuan*. The revised annual exponential growth rate is $[\ln(1779.2) - \ln(362.4)]/20$ or 0.07956, corresponding to an annual growth rate of $\exp(0.07956) = 1.083$ or 8.3 percent. Thus even such a large relative error in the 1998 estimate does not alter the conclusion of a very rapid rate of growth. The reason is that when the estimate for the terminal year is reduced substantially, the effect is averaged out over 20 years in calculating the average rate of growth.

The following considerations may be helpful in evaluating the accuracy of Chinese official statistics. First, it is the stated responsibility of the staff of the Chinese State Statistical Bureau to collect and report data as accurately as possible. The same data are used to construct Five-Year Plans which are openly discussed by members of the Chinese People's Congress and reported in the news all over the world. A critic may recall the years before 1979 when official data were not published regularly as they are today, and the Chinese government could use one set of data for their own planning and another set for the news media. Such practice is long gone. Since 1980, *Statistical Yearbook of China* has been published annually to provide data on all major aspects of the economy. The total output is the sum of the values of outputs of different categories. A critic needs to read the *Yearbook* to find out which component of total output is questionable and by how much the estimate of total output is affected by the error in this component.

Second, I have used the official data to perform many econometric analyses, some of which were reported in Chow (1985, 1994, 2002), and found the results reasonable from the viewpoint of economic theory. The accuracy of the data and the validity of the theory reinforce each other. I have also found honest reporting of data unfavorable to the government. As an illustration, consider the estimate of total number of lives lost during the Great Leap Forward Movement based on official statistics on birth and death rates as I discussed in Chapter 1. The Statistical Bureau is honest in reporting the abnormally high death rates and deficient birth rates during the years of the Great Leap.

Third, is the Statistical Bureau under political pressure to falsify statistics? During the Great Leap Forward Chairman Mao Zedong wanted agricultural output to increase by 50 percent within one year and some villages did report phenomenal increase in output. However the Statistical Bureau made a point to check such unreasonable claims and to report the data accurately. This can be seen by the large reduction in agricultural output and total output from 1960 to 1961. *The Statistical Yearbook of China* reports a reduction of GDP (measured in 1978 prices) from 159.1 billion *yuan* in 1960 to 111.9 billion *yuan* in 1961, in spite of Chairman Mao's urge. In more recent years, Premier Zhu Rongji announced targets for total national output and outputs of particular provinces in 1999, 2000, 2001 and 2002. A provincial governor might have been tempted to falsify data to fulfill the target stated by the premier, but the staff of the State Statistical Bureau in Beijing had all the incentive to correct any falsified statistics reported from below. Premier Zhu would not have tolerated such false reports and would have punished any one liable. One needs to examine the data reported in *Statistical Yearbook of China* carefully before making a general statement that the data are unreliable.

In addition to the three comments above, let me clarify that the rate of economic growth in China might be underestimated by using official statistics because improvement in product quality has not been taken into account. In the United States, the underestimation can take the form of counting one computer produced in 2000 as the same amount of output as one computer produced in 1995 when in fact its quality was much improved. The computer produced in 2000 represents a much larger amount of output because it is faster, has more memory space, etc. The Bureau of Labor Statistics in the US has tried to adjust for quality improvement in constructing its consumer price index. Real output is obtained by dividing nominal output by a price index. Real output is raised by quality adjustment in the price index because the price index in the denominator is reduced. The Chinese State Statistics Bureau has not taken adequate account of the quality

Author's (2nd from left) meeting with President Jiang
(2nd from right) in 1992

improvement in the products produced in China, and thus underestimates the quantity of output in later years as compared with that of (equivalent) output in earlier years. This leads to an underestimation in the rate of growth of real output in China. To the extent that US output data have incorporated quality change and Chinese data have not, a comparison of the US and Chinese output growth rates using available statistics underestimates the relative growth rate of China.

Fundamental Factors of China's Economic Growth

We are justified in projecting substantial economic growth for China in the future if we can identify the factors that have contributed to its growth in the past and it is reasonable to believe that these factors will continue to operate in the future. Since economic reform started in 1978 to transform a planned economy into a market economy, the rate of economic growth in China has been phenomenal. In the first two decades after 1978, the rate of growth of real output, measured by gross domestic product was about 9.6 percent per year on average, as the calculation in the last section demonstrates. As has been pointed out at the end of Chapter 1, there are three fundamental economic forces that have contributed to the rapid economic growth. The first is the high quality of the Chinese people. By high quality I refer to the skills and working ethics of the workers and the energy and resourcefulness of the entrepreneurs. The second is a set of functioning market institutions, even though these institutions have many shortcomings. The Chinese government officials deserve credit in guiding the transformation of the economic system to a market economy, a process described in Chow (2002). The third factor contributing to the rapid growth is that China is a latecomer in economic development. As a late comer it can adopt the new technology and managerial experience that other countries took a long time to develop when they were growing more slowly than China has grown in recent years. These three factors namely, high-quality human capital, market institutions and availability of modern technology for a late comer, were sufficient to generate rapid growth for China as it started from a low level of economic development. Let me turn to these three factors now.

High Quality and Abundance of Human Capital

The importance of human capital for economic development has been mentioned repeatedly in this book. Chinese history and culture as discussed in Chapters 1 and 2 have contributed to the high quality of Chinese human capital. Economic textbooks do not discuss sufficiently the different qualities of the peoples of different nations in affecting the rate of economic development. Because of the high quality of human capital in Germany and Japan, these countries were able to recover rapidly from their low output level at the end of Second World War when much of their physical capital was destroyed. One country's economy can perform better than another country's because the quality of its human capital is better. This fact is generally recognized by economists. However, most economic textbooks emphasizes the number of years of schooling for the measurement of human capital and fail to account for family education and the entire historical tradition of the people involved that can affect their knowledge, motivation and working habits.

The United States is so rich today mainly because of the quality of its people. Compared with the people of most other countries, Americans are highly educated, have managerial skills and have the ability to stay in the forefront of technological innovations. Where else can we find a Silicon Valley? Where else can we find an IBM Thomas J. Watson Research Center, or a Bell Lab before the breaking up of AT&T? Where else can we find universities comparable to the top American universities? These universities provide graduates with sufficient talents to work in the top research organizations and high-tech enterprises in Silicon Valley and elsewhere. It is the quality of the American people, in entrepreneurship, management skills, the ability for scientific and technological innovations, etc. that make America the richest country in the world.

The role of American workers is also important. Since China has an abundance of good-quality and low-cost labor, the manufacturing of many consumer goods, including clothing, shoes, toys, sports equipment, tools and household electric appliances has been moved to China. Competition from the imports of these products in American markets has redirected some American workers to more skilled jobs in high-tech and certain service industries in which the US excels. On the contribution of human capital to China's development, I should mention the overseas Chinese as well. Although they are not Chinese nationals, they have contributed their skills, talents, financial and physical capital and their brainpower towards China's economic development. This is one resource that China has and what other former socialist economies lack.

Market Institutions

The second factor is the Chinese market economy that allows the Chinese workers and entrepreneurs to utilize their talents to better themselves and the nation. I give credit to the Chinese government for successfully transforming the economic system into a market economy. The officials involved in the economic reform were distinguished by their open-mindedness and eagerness to learn from the outside world. They have tried to learn from the experiences of the US, Canada, Japan, Taiwan, other Asian countries, and the Western as well as Eastern European countries. I am not aware of top and mid-level government officials in any other country who have been as willing to learn from the experience of other countries.

The Chinese government officials were pragmatic and willing to try out potentially good ideas to reform the economy on an experimental basis. In 1979 they selected several thousand state-owned enterprises to try out ideas on giving them more autonomy. They used special economic zones to find out ways of absorbing foreign investment, and the areas or cities open to foreign investment were gradually increased. Guangdong province was first allowed to practice market economic policies ahead of other provinces. Once worked out well in an experimental zone, the policy would be implemented elsewhere. The reform process still goes on as of the beginning of the 21st century. Although the Chinese market economy has many shortcomings, including those in the state-owned enterprises and the banking system to be discussed below, the market institutions were good enough to sustain the rapid growth in over two decades after economic reform started in 1978.

The Chinese government also deserves credit for maintaining social stability and law and order, which are necessary for the proper functioning of a market economy.

Availability of Modern Technology to a Latecomer

On the third factor, China has benefited from the technology and management skills acquired from the more developed countries. The main channel through which modern technology and management were introduced into China was foreign investment. Foreign investment also provided the capital needed to construct new factories in which modern technology and management systems were applied. Other economies in Asia, including the economies of Japan, South Korea, Taiwan, Hong Kong and Singapore have succeeded in rapid development using the same three factors of good-quality human capital, market institutions and technology imported from more advanced economies. China is no exception. Since these factors will continue to operate, substantial rates of growth can be expected for China in the next two decades. The rate of growth will be somewhat slower since it was easier for China to grow rapidly from a low output level. China is large, and still has regions that are poor and are capable of rapid growth.

Income Inequality

The rapid economic growth of China was somewhat uneven among different regions. The coastal provinces had higher growth rates than the provinces in the Western region. From the early 1980s to the mid 1990s, the province of Guangdong had the highest growth rate, hovering around 15 percent per year. There were two reasons for Guangdong's very high growth rate. The first is the central government's policy to allow Guangdong to adopt market institutions first. This policy of "one-step ahead" for Guangdong was proposed by Deng Xiaoping as early as 1978 in the 11th Communist Party Congress. Deng envisaged using Guangdong as an experimental station to try out institutions of a market economy. Second, Guangdong is near Hong Kong and could receive foreign investment from and through Hong Kong. Capital, new technology, and new managerial skills were introduced through foreign investment.

The second region to have developed rapidly since the early 1990s is Shanghai. Earlier, Shanghai was heavily taxed by the central government to subsidize the rest of the country. Since the early 1990s the central government has allowed Shanghai to retain more of its output and to adopt market institutions as Guangdong had done. Shanghai's development began to speed up at a phenomenal rate as will be discussed in Chapter 7, which is devoted to the two modern cities of Hong Kong and Shanghai. Fujian and Shandong are two provinces that experienced rapid development in the 1990s, the former partly due to its proximity to Taiwan and the latter to its proximity to Japan and South Korea. In short, the coastal provinces enjoyed higher rates of growth than provinces in the interior, especially the provinces in the Western region.

Since the economic reform started in 1978, regional disparity has increased in China but the rate of increase has slowed down since mid 1990s. This statement is based on an examination of the per capita consumption data of 31 provinces and municipalities through time. The municipalities are Beijing, Shanghai, Tianjin, and Chongqing (added in 1999 to signify its important role in the national program for Western development). One measure of regional disparity is the standard deviation of the logarithm of per capita consumption among the provinces. This standard deviation has increased at the rate of about half of one percentage point per year between 1981 and 1998, but the rate of increase has slowed down to 0.2 of one percentage point in the last five years of this period (Chow, 2002, p. 170). An important fact about China's consumption or income disparity among the people in different provinces is that even the poorest provinces have experienced significant improvement in the standard of living. The province having the slowest improvement between 1981 and 1998 is Guizhou. Its consumption per capita increased by 3.6 percent per year on average during this period (Chow, 2002, p. 169). This is a good record as compared with many other developing economies. The very poor regions of China did benefit from China's economic development although they have improved more slowly than the coastal regions.

Regional disparity has been mitigated substantially by the free movement of the Chinese labor force. Millions of people have moved from the poor regions of the West to the coastal areas, to the benefit of both areas. By migrating, these people have improved their own standard of living and that of their family members, who receive support and remittances from them. They help the economic development of the coastal areas as well. China's national income increases by 250 *yuan* if a worker earning 300 *yuan* in Guizhou moves to Guangdong to earn 550 *yuan* per month. While writing this paragraph I was in Hong Kong during the Chinese Lunar New Year holidays in February 2003. One major topic in the news is the crowded transportation system when millions of immigrant workers in the Pearl River Delta area went home in various parts of interior China to spend their holidays. Extra trips by trains, buses, boats and planes had to be scheduled for these workers, and many of them were allowed to leave early or to come back later to avoid the transportation congestion.

More inequality is commonly perceived to be undesirable. Is increasing consumption or income disparity among different regions necessarily bad? Yes and no. Yes, because the result can be considered unfair, or unjust. It may cause discontent among the poor. Sufficient discontent may cause political stability. No, if the disparity is the result of some regions experiencing more rapid economic development than others are. For example, if the top five percent of the Princeton graduates in a certain year happen to be much better than in a normal year while the remaining 95 percent are only slightly better, there will be an increase in disparity in the starting salaries of Princeton University graduates. Everyone is better off, but the top five percent is much better off.

If the coastal provinces of China can do much better while the remaining provinces are doing somewhat better, it is good for China for two reasons. First, since the coastal provinces are a part of China, their well being is China's well being. Second, they can lead the entire country to become richer. This is the fundamental idea behind the policy of the economic reform in China in the 1980s when the government encouraged some people to get rich first. The country needs an elite to lead the rest in many aspects of economic development. China needs a few top universities, top research centers, successful multinational corporations, and excellent symphony orchestras, among others, to push it forward and to become a highly developed country. This means that some people have to be very rich. The result is increased disparity. Most Chinese welcome the successful and rapid development of Shanghai (see Chapter 7) and are proud of it. The success of Shanghai has not only helped to bring about development of other regions and brought pride to the Chinese, it has increased the regional disparity in China.

The Chinese government considers the development of the poor provinces in the Western region to be very important and has set up a national plan to achieve this goal. The Western region consists of the Chongqing municipality and ten provinces, Sichuan, Guizhou, Yunnan, Tibet, Shaanxi, Gansu, Qinghai, Ningxia, Inner Mongolia, and Xinjiang. The government has tried to build infrastructure for this region, including highways, railroads and power plants. The Three Gorges Project, first launched in 1993 and expected to be completed by 2009, has received much attention around the world. It comprises a set of dams to control the flow of water in the Yangtze River. The main purposes are to control flood, to generate electricity for the region, create jobs and stimulate the local economy. It involves the resettling of many people, some 600,000 by May 2003 and half a million more at a later stage. The May 28 2003 issue of the *People's Daily* reports that by October 2003, 5.5 billion kilowatts/hours of electricity would have been generated by four hydropower-generating units, and by 2009, 18.2 kilowatts/hours would have been generated by 26 power generating units. Some environmentalists object to the project. Other critics say that the problem to remove the expected accumulation of mud in the bottom of the river near the dams has not been solved. I have spoken to a number of knowledgeable people both in China and in the United States (including Princeton faculty members in the engineering school), but have not reached a conclusion on the costs and benefits of this enormous project.

3 Strength and Weaknesses of China's Economic Institutions

One may question whether the Chinese economic institutions are good enough to sustain the rapid growth I have projected above. Many observers have pointed to the weaknesses of China's economic institutions and suggested that although such institutions were good enough to bring China's rapid growth in the past, they cannot sustain the development. There are reasons to think positively. I will examine some of the alleged weaknesses and discuss the possible strength of China's economic institutions.

The Banking System

First let us examine China's banking and financial systems. China's commercial banks have a large number of non-performing loans. Most of these loans have been extended to state-owned enterprises and are unlikely to be repaid. These bad loans can create a problem. In every bank's balance sheets there are assets and liabilities. These loans are assets if they are expected to turn into money in the future. The liabilities are what the bank owes. For Chinese banks, the liabilities include deposits of the Chinese people who have put money in the banks for safekeeping and interest. These are the assets for the depositors and liabilities for the bank. If some loans extended by a bank are bad they cannot be counted as assets to pay the depositors when they withdraw their deposits. When the depositors come to withdraw their money the bank may not have enough assets to pay the depositors. It can go bankrupt. According to the balance sheets of the Chinese banks, many are in such a situation. However these banks are unlikely to go bankrupt because the Chinese banks are different. The bad loans have been accumulated during a period when the banks had to extend credits to state-owned enterprises by order of the economic planning authorities that approved the loans. Sometimes the banks were under political pressure by the provincial government to finance economic development of the province in which the banks are located. Unlike Western commercial banks, where loan officers make loans to borrowers based on credit worthiness, the Chinese banks do not have such autonomy in making their loan decisions. They are still pressured to make loans to state-owned enterprises but begin to have more power to make their own decision.

More importantly, the Chinese people who deposit their money in the banks are not worried that they might lose it. They trust the banks because they know that the banks are owned and backed by the Chinese government. If a bank were to face large amounts of withdraws by depositors, the People's Bank as a central bank could always supply it with enough money to pay the depositors. Since the Chinese people believe that the People's Bank will back up their deposit, they do not need to withdraw the money merely for fear of losing it. Therefore there will not be serious bank runs.

If we look at the total amount of deposits in all the banks in China, we find that it has been increasing at a rapid rate in the last two decades. This has happened because the Chinese people have increased income and they save a large fraction of it, over 35 percent as compared with some five percent in the United States. The banks find their deposits increasing and are not concerned about bank runs. Of course if the central bank has to supply a lot of money to pay the public, the price level may increase, but there is no fear of inflation because the amount of money needed to prevent bank runs is very small. Even if the central bank had to print money to cover all the bad loans in five years, the increase in money supply would still be small relative to the demand for money based on the level of China's GDP, as a simple calculation in Chow (2002, pp. 229–230) shows. In the period of the Asian Financial Crisis of 1997–99 and afterwards, many outside observers expected a banking crisis in China but it did not happen for the reasons I have just stated.

In the meantime, the Chinese government is trying to reduce the amount of bad loans by setting up four Asset Management Corporations to help buy these loans and sell them at a discount. Each asset management corporation is responsible for solving the bad loan problem of one of the four major commercial banks. According to a report in the *People's Daily* of May 29, 2003, at the end of 2002, the weighted average of the non-performing loans in the four banks was 26.12 percent. By the end of March 2003, it had dropped by 1.99 percentage points, or by 17.1 billion *yuan* (3.27 billion US dollars). The problem of non-performing loans is being solved gradually. As another way to reduce the non-performing loans, one can imagine that if the state-owned enterprises owe the banks money but are not able or willing to pay it back, the government which owns the stocks of these enterprises can sell stocks to pay back some of the bad loans. The stocks have value as they are traded in stock markets in Shanghai, Shenzhen, and some even in Hong Kong or New York.

In addition to the problem of the bad loans, the Chinese banks are not efficient in channeling the financial resources at their disposal to productive investment for economic development. The inefficiency is due to the bureaucratic behavior and lack of training of the management and staff of the state-owned commercial banks. This inefficiency has been a drag on China's economic development in the past and will remain so in the near future. The situation can be improved only slowly. Competition from foreign banks under the terms of the WTO (World Trade Organization) will hasten the improvement somewhat during the first decade of the 21st century.

The State Enterprises

Critics often point to the weaknesses of the Chinese state-owned enterprises. They are said to be inefficient and many are operating at a loss. They have also caused unemployment when they lay off many workers. Inefficiency means that they use up a great deal of inputs and produce only little output. The inefficiency of state enterprises may not be a major economic problem for China. First, their role in the production of total output in China has been getting smaller. In the year 2000, state enterprises produced only about 28 percent of China's total industrial output, while the rest was accounted for by collective, private and foreign-owned enterprises. Hence, even if the output growth rate for state-owned enterprises is low, China can still grow rapidly because of the high rate of growth generated by the non-state enterprises. Furthermore, the efficiency of state enterprises has been increasing, although at a slower rate than in the non-state enterprises.

Second, the unemployment problem created by the restructuring of state enterprises has been manageable. In China, state enterprise reform in the late 1990s was the responsibility of the State Economic Commission (now combined into the State Development and Reform Commission). Since state-owned enterprises were under the control of different levels of the Chinese government, from the national government in Beijing to provincial governments and city and township governments, the State Economic Commission at each level was responsible for the restructuring of the state enterprises within its jurisdiction. Each branch commission was in charge of the restructuring of a given set of enterprises using a budget allotted to it. Restructuring of an enterprise required paying the laid-off workers about one third of their regular salaries. Subject to the finite budget allocated for restructuring, the number of enterprises to be restructured in a given year was limited. Thus the Commission staff monitored the speed of restructuring and the extent of unemployment allowed. They were more concerned about the unemployment problem than a foreign observer. The Chinese government wants to make sure that the unemployment situation in each location is not out of control to the point of creating political instability. Unemployment insurance is a part of the social security system that the government is in the process of setting up for the entire country. In the meantime many laid–off workers have been resourceful in finding jobs in a market economy. A tourist can see many stands selling consumer goods along the sides of streets and new shops providing services such as bicycle repair and tailoring.

WTO membership approved in 2001 forces China to accept more foreign competition step by step. Tariffs on agricultural and manufacturing products will be lowered gradually. Foreign firms can enter China's market to produce and to sell more easily. Foreign firms can also enter banking, financial, telecommunication and consulting service sectors of the Chinese economy. Premier Zhu Rongji tried to get China into the WTO in order to invite foreign competition to stimulate the Chinese economy. Some critics are concerned that the Chinese enterprises might not be able to weather severe foreign competition. The story being unfolded in the first decade of China's WTO membership is interesting to observe. Whether and how the Chinese domestic enterprises will be able to survive is difficult to foretell. One development can be expected. If the foreign pressure turns out to be unbearable in a certain situation, there will be delays instituted by the local government, which has the authority to approve the entry of a foreign firm. The central government in Beijing has signed an international agreement but it is partly up to the local authorities to implement that agreement. Local government officials have a fair amount of power in implementing the agreement. A foreign firm following the rules of WTO may find entering the Chinese market more difficult if its entry threatens the existence of local firms.

Moral Basis of China's Legal System

As a third possible weakness of China's economic institutions, consider its legal system. China is alleged to have a weak legal system. China's modern legal system is not well developed yet. The modern Western legal system is a creation of the Western economic development process. Therefore, China's legal system is imperfect as judged by the standards of the legal system of the Western developed economics.

China has had its own legal system for over 2,000 years. During the imperial period, the emperor had the right to decree a set of laws. In the period of the Republic of China, there was a legislature to enact laws that combined elements of traditional Chinese laws and Western legal ideas. The Western legal system may not be the only set of legal institutions that can facilitate economic development. It has worked well for some Western countries, but it may not be the most appropriate system for China. To establish harmony in social and economic conduct, there is a need for a set of rules. People in a market economy cannot function without rules, but rules are not the same as laws. Over 2,000 years ago, the Chinese philosopher Han Fei-tze championed the adoption of a legal system while Confucius taught moral principles. The Chinese choose the use of moral principles as a basis of their legal system perhaps for good reasons. The choice of a set of moral standards over a set of laws as principles of social and economic order, is a difficult topic to discuss. Let me raise the following considerations.

75

In China, moral principles are taught as a part of everyone's principles guiding his or her behavior. Laws are enacted by legislators who have self-interests and are influenced by political pressure. People obey laws partly because there are law enforcement mechanisms. Enforcement of laws is from outside, often by coercion. It is sometimes against a person's will and it limits his freedom. In contrast, Confucius did not choose his teaching of moral principles on the basis of his self-interest as a legislator. He was under no political pressure in writing his principles of social harmony. The practice of a moral code is from within. Once a person accepts the code, he will voluntarily abide by it. Other enforcement mechanism is not required, and the cost of enforcement is spared. Following the same set of moral codes reduces conflicts among different elements of the society. Confucian ethics has lasted for centuries in China because the Chinese believe that it works well. Social order may be better achieved by the practice of a set of moral principles accepted by all than by a legal system that is not firmly grounded on moral values. (Confucian ethics was partly destroyed during the Cultural Revolution of 1966–1976 but has recovered naturally as the effects of the Cultural Revolution gradually subsided. The current government has attempted to reestablish cultural values.)

China's market economy throughout history, especially in the Song dynasty, functioned smoothly by the moral principles of its citizens and without the benefit of a modern legal system. Business conduct in the very dynamic township and village enterprises in the 1980s and 1990s was partly based on a set of social norms that people followed. A gentlemen agreement may be more reliable than a legal contract. There were no high legal fees required to settle disputes. Although the set of rules governing the Chinese township and village enterprises was not perfect, it is difficult to claim that imposing a Western legal system would have been possible and would have improved the situation.

Social Network—*Guanxi*

In a traditional Chinese society, business relations were guided by informal rules governing human behavior. Agreements were enforced and disputes were settled by using such relations known as *Guanxi*. *Guanxi* has several dimensions. To establish *guanxi* with a certain individual, one needs to cultivate his trust and respect. One also accumulates one's own credit and establishes credibility from the eyes of this individual. Such a relationship enables one to get help from the individual when needed. That explains why when a group of Chinese goes out for dinner, everyone fights for the privilege to pay the bill. The person who actually pays accumulates credit in the accounts of all others at the party. The credit can be used when he needs help from the others. People remember and there is no need to keep books. Since some members of the dinner party may have social influence, it is good to establish some credits in their accounts. Things get done through *guanxi*. During the period of central planning when the government controlled the distribution of consumer goods, there was a shortage of consumer goods distributed through government channels. Through *guanxi*, there existed an informal market for people to trade, as described in Butterfield (1982). If you were a pianist you could give piano lessons to the daughter of a doctor and could then go to his home for treatment without having to line up in a public hospital.

In a planned economy, many people had control of assets, both physical assets and human assets including one's own talents. Under socialism, the government owned all major physical assets in name but the people assigned to control the assets could and did use them for their own benefit and trade them for what they needed. A driver of a government-owned vehicle could use it to drive his friends around in exchange for what he needed from them. This institution of informal trades replaced the market for the exchange of goods and services. It was an important aspect of the use of *guanxi* in Chinese societies. Services from professionals such as doctors and piano teachers can be traded for goods or services from others with whom one has established personal relations.

Guanxi also serves to perform some of the functions that a legal system performs. Disputes can be settled through mediation under the system of *guanxi* without the need to settle in court. Even under a legal system disputes are often settled out of court by negotiations between the lawyers. Why ask the lawyers to settle disputes between wife and husband if some relatives or friends who have established *guanxi* with both parties can do the job?

Respect for Patents and Intellectual Property Rights

One aspect of China's legal system in practice is the lack of respect for intellectual property rights. Patent right is a modern invention. It gives the inventor monopoly power in the market of his product. Since the institution of patent right is generally accepted, people may overlook the pros and cons of granting patents. The most often used justification for patent laws is that they protect the inventor from competition and give him a higher return for his effort in innovation, thereby encouraging innovations. The merit of this justification depends on how much effect patent protection has on the effort to innovate, as compared with the harm to the general public when they have to pay a higher price for the protected product. One needs a cost and benefit analysis of the above factors before patents can be justified. We have observed that many innovators in mathematics and science seemed to have done very well without the benefit of patent protection. A pharmaceutical company introducing a new drug already has a big advantage by selling the drug first. One has to balance the incentive effect on its future innovation and the loss to consumers who pay a high price for the drugs. In addition, patents have prevented others from innovating for fear of infringement of existing patents.

Regardless of the pros and cons of patent laws, the Chinese government has accepted them as a necessity. The difficulty of enforcing patent laws in China is due partly to China's historical tradition in addition to the possible economic benefits of violating them. Patent rights did not exist in traditional Chinese societies. Inventors and producers of desirable products protected themselves by keeping the methods of producing the products secret. I have had some personal experience concerning the Chinese attitude towards intellectual property rights. In the 1990s, I gave a lecture in a university in China. A year later a professor of that university, a good friend who had spent two semesters as a visiting scholar in the US, wrote to ask me to comment on an article that he wrote for submission to a journal in China. I was surprised and disturbed when I saw that the article was a set of notes taken from my lecture. Knowing my good friend to be an honest person, I wrote to ask him simply to state in the first paragraph that this is a set of notes taken from my lecture. He accepted my suggestion with thanks. As a second example, a visiting scholar told me in 2002 that she was interested in a topic about the Chinese economy not covered in my textbook. I decided to write up a set of notes and distributed it to my class which she attended. Two weeks later she sent me a paper including paragraphs taken directly from my notes. I was not disturbed because of my earlier experience which I have just described. I simply asked her to use quotes and refer to my notes and she gladly did so. These two incidents have helped me realize that the Western concept of intellectual property rights does not yet exist in China, nor is it being fully understood. Both professors probably thought that they showed respect for me by quoting my work and considered it immaterial whether my authorship was mentioned.

China's Legal and Economic Institutions

The above discussion serves to convey the idea that China's way to preserve social harmony and ensure proper business conduct is different from the Western legal system. Furthermore, patents and intellectual property rights are foreign inventions, which the Chinese have not integrated into their way of thinking. After the establishment of the Republic of China in 1911, the government set up legal institutions modeled after Western countries without interfering with the simultaneous use of moral codes and *guanxi* by the people. In fact the government tried to reinforce the traditional moral and ethical system for the sake of social harmony. It is interesting to observe how the current PRC government deals with the traditional moral system while trying to adopt a modern legal system that suits the purpose of economic development and China's participation in global economic relations.

Since 1978, the record of the PRC government in its effort to modernize the legal system has been impressive. The People's Congress has enacted a large number of laws that are required for the functioning of the market economy. Examples are the Central Bank Law and the Commercial Bank Law, which were enacted in 1995. With the exception of less independence given to the People's Bank, these laws resemble similar ones for the Federal Reserve Bank and the commercial banks in the United States. There are bankruptcy laws, as well as other laws governing corporate behavior, foreign trade and investment, etc. The judicial system has expanded. Supreme People's Court in Beijing has the power to give judicial interpretation of laws. The Litigation Law allows citizens to sue the government. The courts are deciding more cases, including suits against the government. In 1998, there were over 300,000 judicial personnel, including approximately 130,000 judges and 175,000 lawyers. All these developments signaled the modernization of the Chinese legal system.

The impressive record just described should not be interpreted to imply that the Chinese legal system is functioning well. How well the Chinese legal system functions cannot be judged by the number of new laws being enacted or by the number of lawyers, judges, or law suits that have been filed. Formal legislation itself is not sufficient to provide social and economic order. Laws have to be based on moral standards accepted by the population. Some observers suggest that the number of new laws passed by the People's Congress is too large and that the contents of many laws do not take sufficient account of the moral foundation and historical tradition of social behavior, on which all laws must be based. Besides this important point, there are three other possible limitations to the current legal system in China.

First, legal behavior cannot be changed by legislation alone. It is the result of cultural and social tradition. There is inertia in changing social and human behavior. To be law-abiding is a habit that takes time to cultivate. The Chinese have yet to cultivate the habit of going to courts to settle disputes and many do not have high regard for laws. The disregard has been affected by two factors. One is the Cultural Revolution, which lowered people's moral standard and respect for the law for the sake of survival. The other is the experience of economic shortages due to central planning and especially to the failure of the Great Leap Forward Movement. Economic deprivation made the Chinese people more eager to make money when they had opportunities to do so after economic reform. Sometimes money was made by illegal means such as smuggling and selling goods produced in violation of intellectual property rights. In the beginning of the 21st century, there appeared to be signs that, as the country has become richer, the Chinese people were becoming more law-abiding. The government also deserves some credit in promoting orderly social behavior through educational programs besides the reform of legal institutions.

Second, in some respects the effort to introduce Western laws has affected orderly social relations adversely. In traditional Chinese society, such relations are based on the tradition of *guanxi* or social networking. The Chinese consider ethical and moral values more important than laws. They feel justified if they behave properly according to their conscience, which is derived from family education and social values. To the extent that orderly behavior based on such values is disturbed by a legalistic attitude, it may be harmful to society. In a well-recited *Admonitions of Master Zhu*, written as a teaching to his family members, a Confucian scholar in the Qing dynasty advised, "In conducting family affairs, do not quarrel or engage in legal disputes, for engaging in legal disputes will result in misfortune." Many Chinese have followed the above cited advice. Increase in the number of litigations does not imply a better legal and social system. The Western legal system has limitations of its own too. It is said that there are too many lawyers in the United States, and the US economy devotes too much of its resources to legal services.

Third, the Communist Party in its role to provide political leadership is in some sense above the law. Laws cannot be enacted to restrict the power of the Communist Party to rule the country. In practice even when a law applies, the court might decide according to the wish of the government official or Party member who is a party of the dispute.

Chow (1997) under the title *Challenges of China's Economic System for Economic Theory* discusses the role of private versus public ownership, formal versus informal legal system, and individual versus collective welfare. China's experience has suggested that public enterprises, especially the township and village enterprises, can be economically efficient; informal legal institutions can serve the need to enforce business commitments, while the desire for promoting collective welfare (rather than the self interest of an individual) can motivate behavior for the benefit of the economy. Allen, Qian and Qian (2002) consider China as a counterexample to the findings in law and economics that certain forms of Western legal and financial institutions are required for promoting substantial economic growth. Their main point is that while certain Western legal and economic institutions have done well for many economies, they should not be considered the only institutions that can serve the needs of a dynamic market economy. Possibly as a part of their culture, the Chinese tend to believe that there are different ways to solve a problem, including the design of social institutions to foster economic development. Many Chinese even believe in several religions simultaneously.

Market economy has existed in China for a long time, as described by Sima Qian in the Han dynasty. It has evolved through the glorious period of the Song dynasty and by modernization in the first half of the 20th century. After disruptions in the period of central economic planning between the 1950s and 1970s, it has recovered to a large extent. Economic and legal institutions tend to adapt to suit the social circumstances of the population unless a strong government intervenes in the process. Since different countries have different social circumstances, one can expect that their market institutions also differ. It seems inappropriate for economists in the West to refer to some economic institutions in East Asia as "phony capitalism" when several economies in that region were having trouble during the Asian Financial Crisis of 1997–9. Different forms of market and legal institutions may suit the need of different countries. Asian economies have imperfect and non-Western market institutions, but to convert them into certain Western institutions may not be the best way to improve them.

The Chinese People

Who are the Chinese? Are there too many Chinese? These are the two questions I would like to answer. In describing the Chinese people I will consider the Chinese in Mainland China, in Hong Kong, in the United States and in Taiwan with reference to their characteristics. Since their cultural characteristics have been discussed in Chapter 2, this chapter will emphasize the characteristics that have been affected by their recent social environments. On the second question, my conclusion is that China does not have a population problem that requires a strict control of childbirths. This conclusion is not generally accepted and requires careful deliberations.

Who Are the Chinese

The Chinese in Mainland China

There are officially 56 ethnically different groups in Mainland China. The five major groups are Han, Manchu, Mongol, Moslem and Tibetan. Moslems are not a distinct ethnic, but a religious group that may include Hans who believe in Islam. Han is the largest ethnic group and consists of about 92 percent of the total population. Originally from the northeast, the Manchus, who ruled China during the Qing dynasty until 1911, are well integrated into the Chinese society. Originally from the north, the Mongols, who ruled China during the Yuan dynasty, have absorbed the Han culture that was in turn influenced by the Mongolian rule. The Chinese with Moslem background have mostly been socially integrated with the rest of the population. In the schools that I attended in South China in the 1930s and 1940s, there were often one or two Moslem classmates in a class of 25 persons and we did not treat them any differently.

In January 2003, I was teaching a graduate econometrics course in the City University of Hong Kong to 19 students and happened to be lecturing on estimating the effects of different factors on the wage of a worker in China in 1988. According to the study (Chow, 2002, p. 211) that I reported to the class, the wage of a minority (non-Han) urban worker in 1988 was 4.45 percent lower than a Han worker after we allow for the effects of education, experience, gender and communist party membership. As I was commenting on the effect of being a minority on the wage of a worker, I asked whether there was a minority in the class. One student said that she was a Moslem, but she was not practicing the religion seriously. From my own contacts in China, I have observed that the Moslems are integrated into the Chinese society. However those living in the province of Xinjiang in the northwest are majority in their own region and may not agree with the central government on some of its policies. Because of their strong Buddhist tradition, the native people in Tibet in the southwest have not been fully integrated with the rest of China, or with the Han Chinese who have migrated to Tibet. The Chinese government has used much financial and human resource to develop Tibet, but its policy may not have been entirely popular among the native Tibetans.

Besides the five major ethnic groups, there are 51 recognized small ethnic groups in China, each with their own customs and some speaking their own languages. Many can be found in the province of Yunnan in the southwest. Many lead their own ways of life in small areas and are not integrated with the rest of China. They do not feel the need to be integrated, although economic globalization is affecting them in the course of time. There are also immigrants to China, among them are the Jews. The Jewish immigrants are few in numbers and they have concentrated in a few areas, in particular the city of Kaifeng. Many Jewish people in the world are interested in the Jews in China and would like to visit Kaifeng to find out the life of Jews there. From the viewpoint of a Jewish American, the Jews in Kaifeng and in the rest of China are almost completely Chinese in the way they look, the language they speak, the food they eat and their way of life in general.

Ethnic Diversity and Discrimination

That different cultures and ethnic groups make up what China is today is an understatement. The groups have in fact learned from one another to create the distinctive Chinese culture. In many respects, including the use of a common language that the vast majority of Chinese can understand and speak, the groups are integrated, but the integration is not complete. For example, from the study of wage determination of Chinese workers referred to earlier in Chow (2002, p. 211), a minority urban worker earned about 4.5 percent less than his Han counterpart in 1988 while holding other factors explaining the wage rate constant. This is one measure of discrimination against the minority. On the positive side of the integration equation, all groups of Chinese live peacefully together, consider themselves Chinese and most are proud of being Chinese.

To some extent, regional prejudices prevail even among the Han Chinese living in different regions. Here the term "regional" refers mainly to differences in the dialects that the people speak, the kind of food they eat and their social customs. As a person from the province of Guangdong, I was brought up with certain prejudices against non Guangdong people, called "northerners", since Guangdong was located in the extreme south of China. These people spoke a different dialect from mine. Some of their habits were different. After 1949, many people from Shanghai who migrated to Hong Kong felt that the people in Hong Kong discriminated against them by charging them higher prices in local stores. Yet in a few years these people from Shanghai succeeded in establishing textile and other types of industrial enterprises, banks and educational institutions to enrich Hong Kong and have attained high social status in Hong Kong as well. There is a high degree of integration among different ethnic groups in China, but discrimination also exists.

Status of Women

An important aspect of discrimination is the relatively lower status of women in Mainland China. Following the teaching of Confucius, the wife should be a follower of the husband. As an old saying goes, "The virtue of a woman is her lack of talent." This statement presumably implied that an untalented woman could follow her husband better because she would not have independent opinions. Discrimination against women existed in Western countries before woman suffrage. One argument against giving women the right to vote was that their voting would cause family quarrels. These old ideas are no longer consistent with the ideas of modern living.

The status of women has improved a great deal as China began to modernize. School children in the 1930s and 1940s were taught that men and women were equal and the above discriminating quotation was already outdated. Parents sent their kids to school, though there were more boys than girls. Since the foundation of the People's Republic of China, the status of women has continued to improve with economic development. Chairman Mao emphasized the equal status of women in his famous saying, "Women hold up half of the sky." A higher percentage of women participating in the urban labor force results in an increase in urban labor participation rate (the ratio of the number of employed persons to total population) from 32.2 percent in 1957 to 55.2 percent in 1978 (see *Statistical Yearbook of China 1999*, Table 4-1 for data on urban population, and Table 5-4 for the number of employed persons). The government has tried to increase the rate of literacy but the percentage of illiterate women is still higher than that of men. According to *Statistical Yearbook of China 1997* (pp. 76–79), among the population aged 15 and over in 1996, 17.82 percent were illiterate or semiliterate, 10.12 percent among males and 25.54 percent among females. The education levels of men and women are still different.

We can measure discrimination against women by comparing the wage of a female worker with that of a male worker with the same education, experience and other important characteristics affecting the wage rate. According to the study referred to in Chow (2002, p. 211), holding other important factors constant, the wage of a female worker in 1988 was 7.48 percent lower in rural China, and 9.02 percent lower in urban China, than that of a male worker. Presumably it costs the employer 8 or 9 percent more to pay a male worker when employing a female worker could do the same work. If this cost is taken into consideration, as China's market economy becomes more competitive, employers cannot afford to discriminate as much, and the wage differential due to gender difference will in turn decline. This differential between male and female workers was indeed reduced between 1986 and 1992, as shown in Au (2000, pp. 56–57).

Effect of the Cultural Revolution on Behavior

The experience of the Cultural Revolution of 1966–1976 and of the period of economic planning until 1978 has affected the behavior of the Chinese adversely. The Cultural Revolution was perhaps the darkest period in the history of China over 4,000 years. It was a great social chaos. Parents were mistreated by their children, and teachers, by their students, all in the name of a revolution. Red guards who were teenaged followers of Chairman Mao invaded private homes and destroyed private properties that were considered symbols of capitalism or a decadent ancient culture. Many cultural treasures were destroyed. Urban intellectuals were forced to the countryside to live and work with the peasants.

Many suffered a great deal because they were not accustomed to living in the farm. The peasant families who kindly hosted them also suffered because they were unproductive, but they had to be housed and fed. Many intellectuals tried to avoid being sent to the countryside. The survival instinct, which developed during the Cultural Revolution, and to a lesser extent in the economic planning period when there were shortages of consumer goods, has led some Chinese to be deviant. They have learned how to "beat the system" in order to survive. Such negative experience has colored the behavior of many Chinese people even though they have benefited from a long cultural tradition of moral behavior.

Here are some examples of Chinese behavior to "beat the system." Students from China arrived in Princeton University in the early 1980s, only several years after the end of the Cultural Revolution in 1976. There were reports that some Chinese students broke the code to use the Princeton phone system to make long-distance calls to China free of charge. Some have managed to make up false documents such as course grades and letters of recommendations from well-known Chinese universities to gain admission to Princeton. Others applied to study sciences because there were programs to support Chinese students in certain areas, including physics, biology and statistics. They had intended to change to another field such as economics or business administration to make money, even before leaving China. They applied to the designated field only as a stepping stone and did not consider it unethical. As educators in the United States, we encourage our students to change fields if the change suits their interests the best. But the Chinese students who intentionally used admission to one field as a stepping stone to get into another field is a different matter. One top university had a program to help train Chinese statisticians. After several years, all Chinese students in that program had transferred to other fields, leaving the director of that program disappointed. After spending his research grant money, he did not train a single PhD from China for several years.

In the period of the tragic Tiananmen incident of June 4, 1989, many examples of misbehavior can be cited. In Princeton in August 1989, I had dinner with a group of about ten students from China, to celebrate the completion of a PhD in economics by one student. In discussing Tiananmen, one student suggested that they should spread rumor about once or twice a month that one Japanese was killed in China to create trouble for the Chinese government even if no Japanese were killed. One Chinese student at Harvard actually spread a rumor that Premier Li Peng was shot and this rumor was later found to be false.

Similar, or worse behavior can be found among Chinese student leaders who had demonstrated in Tiananmen Square. The best known leader was found to be a playboy, who fled to the United States, using the money intended for promoting democracy in China to buy expensive clothes and to spend lavishly with women. Another well-known leader later admitted that she was lying when she held the microphone in Tiananmen Square to announce that many students were being killed by tanks. She said that blood shed was needed to promote the course of democracy. Perhaps announcing bloodshed dishonestly was a way to promote blood-shed. It was other people's blood that she was referring to because she managed to get out and come to the United States.

I myself was fooled by such announcements of killing of students by the tanks in Tiananmen Square. A friend in Hong Kong gave me tapes of scenes of Beijing during the Tiananmen incident. He had recorded them when they were broadcast on TV. After watching the tapes for hours, I was sure of the killing of students in Tiananmen Square. Later I brought this up to President Jiang Zemin when I met with him in August 1989. When President Jiang asked me to produce the evidence I went home to look at the tapes again. I realized that there were only voices of announcers describing the killing of students on the square but saw no pictures. Many people saw from TV the killing and injury of citizens, students and soldiers along Changan Street, where citizens blocking

Meeting with President Jiang Zemin (right) in 1989

the tanks from entering Tiananmen Square came into conflict with the military personnel, but the killing of students in Tiananmen Square by tanks was based only on voice announcements. A TV documentary from PBS (Public Broadcasting Service) later showed that the students were wise enough to retreat from Tiananmen Square when the tanks slowly moved in to disperse them.

4 *Abuse of Economic Power*

American and other foreign investors in China can tell stories about the ways Chinese bureaucrats have tried to extract money or favors from them. An agreement signed in Beijing requires the approval of many bureaus. Then the local officials will get their cut. Negotiation is difficult because each time an investor thinks that the deal is closed, he would find out that the Chinese want more. I have discussed the opportunities and problems for foreign investors in China in Chow (2002, Section 18.5), where I commented on the behavior of the Chinese in trying to extract more from foreign investors. Such behavior has been affected by the "need to survive" experienced during the Cultural Revolution and the period of material shortages created by central economic planning.

In Chapter 6, I will discuss corruption and explain how economic temptation has led to corruption on the part of Chinese bureaucrats. As a general observation, people's behavior is affected by the environment. The system of economic planning itself induced the Chinese to take full advantage of the assets at their disposal. Under the system of central planning, most of the economic assets in China were owned by or under the control of the government, since private property was essentially abolished. However all assets had to be managed by people since the government had to assign some people to control and use the assets on its behalf and in the name of the state. In reality the people managing government assets used them for their own benefits. Corruption was only one example when the bureaucrats controlling some economic assets extracted money from people who desired to use the assets. A driver of a government-owned car could use the car for personal benefits. If another person had wanted to use the car, he would have to compensate or appease the driver since there were no cabs available.

Under the system of central planning when all important assets were controlled publicly and consumer goods were not available in the market place, two phenomena occurred. First, the Chinese people became frustrated when they had to beg to get served or to acquire the essential consumer goods. They then aired their frustrations and returned the favor to others when other people needed goods and services from them. The quality of services provided in China was poor in general. People were unkind to one another. The person in control would not readily grant another the needed asset or service. Second, barters became widespread. A person in charge of selling low-price and scarce theatre tickets could exchange the tickets for scarce consumer goods distributed in government stores, as already discussed in Chapter 3 under the subject of *guanxi*. With the appearance of the market economy, the quality of services provided by the Chinese people has gradually improved, and the people have been kinder to one another. Now money can be used to buy goods and services and fewer people have monopoly control of economic resources that others need.

Before I end my discussion on the bad behavior of some Chinese, I would like to return to the positive side. For every bad story that I have about the Chinese students in the United States I can tell at least 50 good ones. Many professors in American universities are impressed by and proud of the students from China. Many Chinese students are truly outstanding in various fields and have high moral standards. Most have graduated and got good jobs in the United States or China, or have succeeded in their own businesses or professions. On the experience of foreign investors who have to deal with Chinese bureaucrats, there is sufficient favorable experience for many to return and to increase their investment. The inflow of foreign investment has been increasing by over 10 percent per year in the five years up to 2002.

Chinese Outside of Mainland China

Overseas Chinese in General

There are Chinese all over the world. Most of them have retained their cultural tradition in varying degrees and in various ways as they adapt to the environment of the country they now reside in. Many of them have a sense that they are Chinese. They think about their home country, although less so when the PRC government closed the door of China and put into practice a political and economic system that they disliked. The concept of a "home village" is important in Chinese thinking. It is not where a person was born, not necessarily where his father, his grandfather and even his great grandfather were all born and lived, but where his ancestors originated. My paternal family had moved from Jiangxi province to Guangdong about six generations ago, but my father told me that my "home village" was a certain town in Jiangxi province and I should consider myself a Jiangxi person. Perhaps the idea of belonging to some village back home is in the mind of many Chinese abroad. In recent years, we learn of second and third generation Chinese Americans visiting their "home village" in China to find their roots.

Many of the overseas Chinese, a term used in China no matter what their nationalities are, still speak Chinese. Some can read and write Chinese very well, including those living in Singapore. Some even practice the customs and way of life prevailing in China decades ago more thoroughly than those living currently in Mainland China, which has been changing rapidly. Naturally the overseas Chinese also adopt new ways of life to adapt to the environment of the area or country they reside in. I will discuss the Chinese in Hong Kong, in the United States and in Taiwan in turn.

Chinese in Hong Kong

In the 1930s almost the entire population of Hong Kong were people from the bordering Guangdong province, who chose to live in this British Colony. The British had introduced a Western style market economy and a modern legal system in Hong Kong. The population of Hong Kong numbered only about 600,000, much smaller than that of Guangzhou (Canton in English at the time), the provincial capital of the Guangdong province. Migration in and out of Hong Kong was completely free. The fact that not many people had moved to Hong Kong suggests that the economic conditions provided by the market economy of China at the time were sufficiently attractive to many Chinese living in Guangdong province and elsewhere in China. Of course people do not decide on the place of residence by considering economic opportunities alone, but a big difference in economic opportunities as existed after the establishment of the PRC in 1949 would and did cause an exodus to Hong Kong.

The British colonial government deserves credit in providing the Chinese residents in Hong Kong with economic opportunities. This statement can be made without having to compare the relative merits of the market economic institutions in Hong Kong and in Guangzhou in the 1930s. Under the British colonial rule, the Hong Kong people seemed to have developed some special characteristics. They are law-abiding, good in business and making money, less interested in intellectual pursuits for their own sake, and were not concerned or involved in political activities. Some of these characteristics have changed somewhat since the return of Hong Kong's sovereignty to China in 1997.

The British set up a well-functioning legal system in Hong Kong and helped the residents develop a sense of respect for the law. By and large, the Hong Kong people are law-abiding. One important institution to note is the Independent Commission Against Corruption established in the 1974 that practically eliminated corruption prevailing at the time and is still playing an important role in preventing corruption by government officials. The Hong Kong people take corruption seriously and know that they have this remarkable institution in the government to fight it. In the 1960s and early 1970s government corruption was fairly widespread. I recall one visit to Hong Kong in the 1960s. My brother was a practicing architect. I accompanied him to buy an expensive gold gift for the British government official in charge of approving the plans for his housing projects. Such bribery was quite common at the time in order to get things done. To deal with one important case of police corruption in 1973 the people urged the government to establish a Commission to stop such corruption. Offenders were to be exposed and punished severely. Corruption was indeed stopped. Perhaps there is an important lesson to learn from the Hong Kong experience on how to fight corruption. One aspect of the solution that the Mainland China government cannot easily adopt is the very high salaries of Hong Kong civil servants that help to reduce the incentive for corruption.

The Hong Kong people are good at making money. They are good workers and competent entrepreneurs. They work in a fast pace, without wasting any time or opportunity to get rich. They are efficient. Up to the early 1950s the Hong Kong business people worked mainly in commercial and financial establishments. Industry expanded after the influx of immigrants from Shanghai in the 1950s. The Shanghai immigrants contributed to the quality of human capital in Hong Kong. Since the 1950s people in Hong Kong have become successful not only in commercial and financial but also in industrial enterprises. They have gained experience in construction during the real estate booms generated by the influx of immigrants from Mainland China. Since 1978 they have shared their financial and human capital with Mainland China by investing in industrial, commercial and construction enterprises there.

Hong Kong is a commercial city with a commercial culture. It has been observed by professors in Hong Kong that Hong Kong students in the universities are much less motivated to study as an intellectual pursuit than the students from the mainland or studying in the universities in the mainland. A large fraction of university students in Hong Kong do not really care about learning for the sake of acquiring knowledge. They are interested in studying subjects that they consider useful for making money quickly. Most would like to get a college degree as a means to get rich. In general, Hong Kong people seem to take money more seriously than people do elsewhere. A person's social status is determined almost entirely by his wealth. If one person were worth 2 billion US dollars, as this applies to some Hong Kong people, he/she would be considered better than a person worthy of only 1.5 billion would. Social stratification is based on wealth. If a person goes out with someone having twice his wealth, he tends to yield to the richer person. These statements might be somewhat exaggerated in order to convey the meaning of a commercial culture. This culture has changed somewhat because, given self-rule, social status is also conferred by a high position in the government and by political connections.

Under the colonial rule, people in Hong Kong did not participate actively in the government, and had little interest in politics. Hong Kong did not have a democratic government. The Hong Kong governor was appointed in London. With the change of government in 1997, the Hong Kong people still lack the experience to govern themselves. Previously they concentrated on making money, leaving the governance to the British. Under the "one country two systems" policy of the PRC government, Hong Kong is ruled by Hong Kong people, who meet a legal requirement of residency in Hong Kong for seven consecutive years. The Beijing government cannot send or support a non-resident to govern this special administrative region (SAR). As 1997 approached the British government promoted some civil servants to higher posts, up to the position of secretary (cabinet member of the government) that had previously been reserved mainly for the British. A small number of high-ranking Chinese civil servants learned quickly to assume responsibility, while others learned more slowly and were good only in taking orders from the British and not in making major decisions on their own. Members of the entire cabinet were re-appointed to serve the new government in 1997. It was very unfortunate that the Asian Financial Crisis of 1997–99 occurred almost immediately after the change of sovereignty. Economic policies of the new government contributed to the economic downturn (of over 3 percent in 1998) in Hong Kong following the financial crisis, as many observers have noted. During the same period, Mainland China and Taiwan were able to maintain a substantial rate of growth.

As of the spring of 2003, according to public opinion polls, the Hong Kong people were dissatisfied with the SAR government. A number of government policies could have contributed to this unpopularity. To cite a few examples, the announcement on July 1, 1997 to increase the supply of public housing units by 85,000 per year depressed the Hong Kong housing market. Along with later policies on housing including the sale of government housing units at below market prices, it contributed to the decline of housing price to the point where many apartment units are worth less than the outstanding mortgage loan. The policy to force all schools teaching English as the basic language to switch to Chinese deprived the parents the freedom to choose the type of schools. It destroyed a well-functioning primary education system with two types of schools and lowered the level of English proficiency in Hong Kong. Big projects were initiated to develop Hong Kong into a major center for science/technology and for high-tech industries when the conditions were not suitable, leading to the abandonment or postponement of such projects. An attempt to merge two well-established major universities into one received strong oppositions from educators. The reorganization of the executive branch of the government by introducing a layer of bureaucrats above the existing secretaries created administrative confusion and resistance.

Before gaining sufficient experience, a better policy for the Hong Kong government to follow would be to keep the previous system intact as much as possible without trying new and unproven ideas. All the policy failures cited above were deviations from the existing system. Hong Kong had a good system going in 1997. However, there is one complication. The last colonial governor had changed the system by introducing elements of democracy and reducing the power of the executive branch of the government, for better or for worse. It has become more difficult for the new government to govern. More democracy may be a good thing but the British government did not have to deal with the problems associated with it. On the positive side, Hong Kong's experience in introducing democratic institutions may be useful for the implementation of political reform in the mainland and towards a more democratic government.

Do the people in Hong Kong consider themselves Chinese? Before 1997, some people in Hong Kong did not consider themselves Chinese. They called themselves "Hong Kong people." Many were concerned that the change of sovereignty would destroy their way of life. Thousands moved to Canada if they could afford it. After 1997, as conditions in Hong Kong turned out to be better than many had expected, a large number of people moved back to Hong Kong from Canada and elsewhere. Some of the people who used to identify with the British colonial rule have changed their mind and now consider themselves Chinese. Today almost all Hong Kong people have accepted the fact that Hong Kong is a part of China and that they are Chinese.

Chinese in the United States

There have been waves of emigration of Chinese to the United States. Before the Second World War, waves of Chinese had emigrated to America in spite of the very restrictive policy against Chinese immigrants in the first part of the 20th century. One group came as workers helping to build railroads in the West in the later part of the 19th century. The poor Chinese tended to migrate when economic conditions in China were very bad. The early Chinese immigrants became workers, with some changing their occupations to become restaurant or laundry owners. Successful ones went on to other businesses. Most lived in Chinatowns in major cities. After the Second World War, a number of students including myself came to the United States to study, but chose not to return because of the Communist rule in China. Then people from Taiwan and Hong Kong came during the 1950s to the 1970s. The students from Hong Kong were small in number and many returned to Hong Kong. Many students from Taiwan still remained in the United States, but some have returned to Taiwan in recent years. The last wave of Chinese immigrants came after the PRC opened its doors in 1979. Many are still residing in the United States.

The groups of Chinese immigrants, before the Second World War, after the Second World War up to the 1970s and after 1979, are different because of their different backgrounds. But they all had to adjust to the American way of life from a Chinese cultural background. This is true not only for the first-generation Chinese Americans. The second and third generations have to deal with relations with their parents and grandparents who had been more heavily influenced by the Chinese cultural tradition. Consider the relation between the children and their first or second generation Chinese-American parents. Some were taught to speak a Chinese dialect as their first language and had to learn English in kindergarten or first grade. As they grew older their parents tried to teach them how to behave as a child in a Chinese family — to be modest and not to boast, to respect the teacher by listening more and asking few questions, to be disciplined rather than to act freely and so forth. The child would soon find out that he is different from the majority of his schoolmates. Cultural differences at home are intensified by racial difference. The child soon discovers that he looks different and is sometimes teased by his classmates. He would ask himself, "Am I a Chinese or an American?" He is not quite an American because he looks different and his parents are different in thinking and behavior from the majority Americans. He is not a Chinese. If he were, he would be afraid that his schoolmates might not accept him as one of them. He would be an outsider. This identity crisis is facing many a young Chinese American.

It took me a long time, after our first child had gone to college, to realize that such an identity crisis is quite common among Chinese Americans (and perhaps other Asian-Americans as well). I had no such identity crisis when I grew up in China. When I grew up, I did not have to face the situation as has been described above. I felt slightly uneasy as a foreign student when I first arrived at the United States because I could not speak English easily and did not know many American customs. (I recall one small incident: A classmate who was a veteran of Second World War asked me to babysit for him. I was happy to help out, reading my book while the baby was asleep. When the parents came home, my classmate tried to pay me for the service. I absolutely refused. How could I accept money from a friend for such a service? There was a big argument between us.) When our first child grew up I did not realize that he was experiencing an identity problem like other Chinese-American children. He did not talk to us about it. Or he might have hinted it to us on occasions but we were oblivious to such a possibility.

With or without identity problems, many second and third generations Chinese-Americans are now living happily and productively. From the perspective of many European-Americans, young Asian-American students present serious competitions for their children in school. Many Asian-American children are asked by their parents to work hard in their academic work, and some have succeeded not only in school but also in national competitions in mathematics and science. Even today, some Chinese-American parents were influenced by what they had been taught in China to ask their children to get ahead in society and to study subjects that will improve their social and economic status. At Princeton, Chinese-American students have told me that their parents wanted them to study medicine, science or engineering, rather than history or literature, for the purpose of earning a good living. I would have to convince such parents, given an opportunity to speak to them, that in the United States, one can be happy and earn a decent living no matter what his field is and that a student will do the best by choosing a major that he or she likes.

Chinese-Americans have contributed to different aspects of American life and there is no need for me to discuss their contributions in this book. However, I will mention their contributions to China. Like the Chinese people in Hong Kong and in other parts of the world, they have contributed a great deal to the modernization and economic development of Mainland China. They have contributed both financial and human capital to China's development. Chinese-American scientists, educators, entrepreneurs and professionals have helped in China's modernization by lecturing, consulting, advising, developing and investing in joint projects with their Chinese counterparts and with the Chinese government.

Chinese in Taiwan

The vast majority of people living in Taiwan can trace their ancestry to China. They speak a dialect spoken by people in a certain area in Fujian Province across the Taiwan Strait, from which their ancestors migrated to Taiwan. They use the Chinese written language. They have essentially a Chinese culture. Do the people consider themselves Chinese? Some do and some do not. Those who consider themselves Chinese may not necessarily wish to be citizens of the People's Republic of China, at least not today.

As I understand the history, many people in Taiwan welcomed the return of the island to Chinese rule in 1945 after it had been seceded to Japan at the end of the Sino-Japanese War of 1891. Most people rejoiced in the return of the island to the motherland. Unpopular deeds of the government under President Chiang Kai-shek alienated the people in Taiwan. From the 1960s to the 1980s Taiwan experienced rapid economic growth under the government of the Republic of China controlled mainly by people who had come to Taiwan from the mainland with Chiang. However, many people born in Taiwan were unhappy with the Chiang government because of his earlier mistreatment of native Taiwanese and of the insufficient representation of native Taiwanese in the government. The deeds of the PRC government in Mainland China at least up to the 1980s did not engender affection or a sense of belonging from the Taiwan population. With this historical background, many people in Taiwan do not feel that Taiwan is a part of China, at least not a part of the People's Republic of China. Some people in Taiwan, especially those who had migrated to the island with Chiang and their family members, feel that they are Chinese and would prefer having closer political ties with the PRC government. Some native Taiwan people, including the leading entrepreneur Y. C. Wang, Chairman of Formosa Plastics, would like to come to terms with the PRC government including the continuation of a dialogue on the issue of a political union under the premise of "one China" that the PRC government demands.

Whatever the course of political integration between both sides of the Taiwan Strait will be, economic integration has taken place rapidly. Taiwan was the third largest foreign investor for Mainland China, next only to Hong Kong and Japan, until 1998 when the United States took its place. The people on both sides of the Taiwan Strait are friendly to each other. Many Taiwan people have a second home in Mainland China. It is estimated that some 300,000 Taiwanese have settled in Shanghai alone. For the critics who think that China does not have sufficient human rights and individual freedom, the presence of these immigrants from Taiwan may help alleviate their concern.

Will continued economic integration lead to some form of political integration? In the very short run up to June 2003, the two sides have not even resumed their semi-official dialog after President Li Teng-hui of Taiwan announced in March 1999 that negotiation had to be conducted on a "state-to-state" basis. The PRC government considers Taiwan a province of China and is not willing to negotiate on a "state-to-state" basis. The situation as of June 2003 is that the PRC government insisted that the Taiwan government accept the principle that there is only one China before formal negotiations could resume, but the Taiwan government has not accepted this principle.

In the longer run, within ten to 15 years, many observers believe that the status quo will continue and Taiwan will continue to be politically independent. I believe that political integration will take place only if the people in Taiwan are willing. Here I assume that the PRC government will not use force to achieve political integration. The use of force is unlikely because (1) the PRC government realizes that it is too costly and risky to use force, although it has not openly ruled out the use of force for the purpose of political unification, as that would weaken its bargaining position; (2) the PRC government is preoccupied with its major task to modernize China and would be concerned with unfavorable international reactions to its use of force; (3) the Taiwan government has considerable air and naval power to protect itself; and (4) the United States would be in the position to intervene if the PRC government were to use force. Readers can form their own judgment on this issue. Some observers think that the Chinese government is irrational and can be reckless. Hence the Taiwan situation is explosive.

Other than by the use of force, the only course for unification is for the people and the government of Taiwan to agree on some form of political integration. I cannot think of any form that the Taiwan government would prefer to the status quo. In what ways can some form of political integration benefit the Taiwan people and government? Any person predicting political integration within the next 15 years has to come up with an answer to this question. Closer economic integration is not an answer. The EU (European Union) countries are economically integrated, and the United States and Canada are also economically integrated. Yet the countries involved are not politically integrated. Each country preserves its own political identity. Most people in Taiwan would like to preserve their own political identity. However, it is possible that one day in the future when the PRC is so rich, its government is so popular, and it has attained such a high status in the community of nations that the Taiwanese would feel proud to be citizens of PRC. But that day is unlikely to come within 15 years.

China's Population Problem

China's population is over 1.3 billion in 2003, the largest among all nations. India takes the second place, having about 800 million people. The United States has about 280 million, about one fifth of China's. Is such a large population a problem for China, or is it a blessing?

There are numerous concerns about China's large population that need to be addressed. Let me first consider a concern that such a large population may create a food shortage for the world. This concern can be easily dispelled. China is essentially self-sufficient in food, with its export and import of food roughly balanced. Even if China were a net importer, there would be no food shortage for the world as a whole. As the world's population increased in the last century, technology improved and investment in agriculture increased to produce more food per capita for the world as a whole. Improvement in technology and investment in agriculture can create more food per person in the future, with due allowance for the proper protection of the environment, as is now generally recognized. In a world of economic specialization, some countries like Japan are food importers while others are food exporters. As long as total supply of food in the world is abundant, as the historical trend of economic development suggests it to be, any country deficient in food production can buy food in the world market if it can afford it. China's per capita income is more than sufficient for this purpose. The shortage of food, if it exists, is not in the total world supply but is a concern for countries or people that are too poor to afford it. China's continued economic development will benefit these countries, not only because of the foreign assistance policy of the Chinese government but also of the possible increase in demand for exports of their product in the Chinese market.

The Chinese Government Considers a Large Population a Problem

Let me turn to the concerns from the viewpoint of China's own economic development. There is a common belief in China that the very large population is a liability for the nation. The Chinese government shared this belief when it introduced family planning in 1971. The policy encouraged late marriages, longer intervals between births, and a smaller number of children per family. These measures were mild as compared with the "one couple, one child" policy introduced in 1980. When the one-child policy was introduced, there was a popular educational campaign via mass media to provide information about family planning and to encourage the practice of birth control. Economic rewards were given for practicing good family planning and economic penalties were applied to those who did not follow the policy. Chinese newspapers reported cases of drowning of female infants in rural areas and abnormally high ratios (larger than one) of the number of male births to the number of female births in certain counties (see Chow, 2002, pp. 187–8). The preference for male children together with the one-child family policy resulted in cases of reported infanticide. In the late 1980s, the policy was relaxed somewhat for the rural families as they were allowed to have a second child if the first-born was a female, but the policy continues up to the present.

Before 1971, China did not have a policy for family planning. In fact in the late 1950s, Chairman Mao Zedong of China's Communist Party said, "A large population is a good thing." Although Chairman Mao had his reasons for favoring a large population, which might be different from mine to be explained below, I tend to agree with his conclusion.

How Many Chinese Are Too Many

When people consider China's population to be too large, what are their possible concerns? One is the high population density, the number of persons per unit of land or per square mile. By this measure, China is not as densely populated as Japan, Taiwan and most European countries. These countries do not seem to have a population problem. Another is with the number of people per square mile of cultivated land. In 1980, when the one-child family policy was introduced, China had 0.27 acre of cultivated crop land per person as compared with 0.12 acre for Taiwan, although the climate and soil condition in Taiwan were probably better for food production. Many areas that have much higher population densities than China, such as my home state New Jersey, are not considered to have excessive population. Why do we think that China has too many people? Besides population density another consideration is that China is poor, much poorer than New Jersey in terms of per capita income. Can China become richer by having fewer people?

The answer is no. At first glance it might seem that having fewer mouths to feed in a family means more food per person. Consider a Chinese family of two children, supported by two working parents each earning 400 *yuan* per month. If the family size is reduced to three by having only one child, at first glance there seems to be an improvement. Per capita income will increase from 200 to 800/3 or 267 *yuan*. But there are two reasons why this improvement is not true. The family may now be richer in per capita terms than before, but in the future when the parents become old, an extra child could provide more income to each of them. This statement holds when there is social insurance to provide for the retired, because for the society as a whole, working people (children of today) will be needed to produce to support the retired. The higher the ratio of working people in the future (children of today) to the retired people (working people of today), the more will each retired person get in the future. What may seem to be an economic liability of today, in the cost of raising children, will turn out to be an economic asset of tomorrow, in the form of output produced by the children after they grow up. Having children is a form of investment. One has to use resource to build a commercial building today in order to collect rent from it in the future. China or any other country has to put in resources to raise children today in order to get working people to produce in the future. Children may be an economic liability of today, but they will be an economic asset of tomorrow.

Secondly for the measurement of the family's well being today we should not treat children only as an economic liability for the parents. They provide joy and satisfaction to the parents. Even if they do not provide support for the parents in the future, many parents consider the fun and joy of today alone by having them to be well worth the expenses required. Only the parents know how much enjoyment they get in having one more child at their home. Outsiders are in no position to tell them that they have too many children as long as they are willing to support the children. Like people in other countries, the Chinese may want more children because of the joy of having them and because of the future security that they can provide. Some Chinese families may be poor, but they should decide for themselves whether to use their limited financial resources to support an additional child.

Can China Afford to Have More Children

An advocate for population control in China may think that having a larger family is not merely a family matter, but a possible burden for the society, and thus a matter of national policy. Some have suggested that China is so poor that it cannot afford more children. This statement is not supported by the reality of China, even if we do not consider the need for having children as an investment for China's future. Whether China can afford having more children, or a faster population growth, depends on how fast China's economy is growing and by how much a faster population growth would slow down the rate of economic growth per capita. In the two decades after 1978, China's real output was growing at 9.6 percent per year on average. Before the one-child policy was introduced in 1980, the birth rate was about 18.2 per thousand population per year, while the death rate was about 6.3 per thousand, yielding a natural growth rate (the difference) of about 11.9 per thousand (see Table 4.1). If the population growth rate equaled this pre-control growth rate of 1.19 percent per year, or were as high as the rate 1.57 percent in 1975, the per capita GDP of China in the two decades after 1978 would still have grown by a phenomenal rate of 9.6 minus 1.6 or more than 8 percent because more people produced more output. Thus the rate of output growth was high enough to absorb any reasonable increase in population without the intervention of the one-child family policy.

Consider the situation in the late 1990s. China's real output was growing at a rate of about 8.1 percent per year while the rate of population growth was about 0.9 percent per year (see Table 4.1), yielding an annual rate of output growth per capita of 8.1 minus 0.9 or 7.2 percent, which is a very high rate. If the government were to allow the people to have as many children as they desired, and if the resulting rate of population growth were similar to the rate of 1.2 percent in 1980 before the one-child family policy was introduced, the rate of growth of per capita output would have been reduced to more than 8.1 minus 1.2 or 6.9, still a very high rate. Even if the birth rate or the rate of increase in population (the death rate being the same) were raised by as much as 0.3 percentage point above the pre-control rate of 1.2 percent, the rate of output growth would still be as high as 6.6 percent per year. China's economic growth is fast enough to afford a higher rate of population growth without the need of population control.

Is it reasonable to assume that, absent the one-child policy, China's birth rate in 1998 would not have been raised from its actual 16 per thousand to more than the 1980 figure of 18.2 plus another 3.0 per thousand as has been suggested in the above calculations? (Readers who are satisfied with the analysis and conclusion reached above may skip this and the following paragraph.) This assumption is very reasonable and conservative because economic forces at work would by themselves lower the birth rate in 1998 as compared with 1980. Let us examine some data provided in *Statistical Yearbook of China* as reproduced by Chow (2002, p. 184) and in Table 4.1. These data suggest that the birth rate is determined mainly by economic factors and that government policy on birth control has only a limited effect on it. Table 4.1 shows that China's birth rate in the cities declined drastically from 44.48 per thousand population per year in 1957 to 14.17 in 1980. This drastic reduction in the birth rate occurred without the intervention of a one-child family policy. Before 1970, the Chinese government did not discourage the people from having children. In 1971 the Chinese government started a mild birth control program to encourage late marriage and discourage people from having a large family. Yet the birth rate had already decreased

Knowing China

Table 4.1 Annual birth rate, death rate, and natural growth rate of the Chinese population, 1952–98

Year	National			City			Country		
	Birth Rate	Death Rate	Natural Growth Rate	Birth Rate	Death Rate	Natural Growth Rate	Birth Rate	Death Rate	Natural Growth Rate
1952	37.00	17.00	20.00	44.48	8.47	36.01	32.81	11.07	21.74
1957	34.03	10.80	23.23	35.46	8.28	27.18	37.27	10.32	26.95
1962	37.01	10.02	26.99	26.59	5.69	20.90	39.53	10.06	29.47
1965	37.88	9.50	23.38	21.30	5.35	15.95	31.86	7.57	24.29
1971	30.65	7.32	23.33	14.71	5.39	9.32	24.17	7.59	16.58
1975	23.01	7.32	15.69	13.56	5.12	8.44	18.91	6.42	12.49
1978	18.25	6.25	12.00	14.17	5.48	8.69	18.82	6.47	12.35
1980	18.21	6.34	11.87						
1985	21.04	6.78	14.26						
1986	22.43	6.86	15.57						
1987	23.33	6.72	16.61						
1988	22.37	6.64	15.73						
1989	21.58	6.54	15.04	16.73	5.78	10.95	23.27	6.81	16.46
1990	21.06	6.67	14.39	16.14	5.71	10.43	22.80	7.01	15.79
1991	19.68	6.70	12.98	15.49	5.50	9.99	21.17	7.13	14.04
1992	18.24	6.64	11.60	15.47	5.77	9.70	19.09	6.91	12.18
1993	18.09	6.64	11.45	15.37	5.99	9.38	19.06	6.89	12.17
1994	17.70	6.49	11.21	15.13	5.53	9.60	18.84	6.80	12.04
1995	17.12	6.57	10.55	14.76	5.53	9.23	18.08	6.99	11.09
1996	16.98	6.56	10.42	14.47	5.65	8.82	18.02	6.94	11.08
1997	16.57	6.51	10.06	14.52	5.58	8.94	17.43	6.90	10.53
1998	16.03	6.50	9.53	13.67	5.31	8.36	17.05	7.01	10.04

dramatically from 44.48 per thousand in 1957 to 21.30 in 1971. The dramatic decline to 21.30 in 1971 could not have been the result of a population control policy which did not exist. The decline from 44.48 in 1957 to 14.71 in 1975 can be explained by the large increase in the percentage of women participating in the labor force, leading to an increase in the overall labor participation rate in urban areas from 32.2 percent in 1957 to 55.2 percent in 1978. Working women did not have time to bear and care for children.

Now consider the city birth rate after 1980, it increased from 14.17 per thousand in 1980 to 16.73 in 1989, during a period when the one-child policy was introduced to the urban population. Increase in economic prosperity, especially in the countryside, which overshadowed the effect of the one-child policy can explain this increase. Between 1989 and 1998, the city birth rate was reduced to 13.67 per thousand while the national birth rate was reduced to 16.03 per thousand. This happened without a change in policy, and can be accounted for by a higher degree of urbanization in China. (The above economic explanations of the changes in birth rate, per thousand total population, from one year to another have ignored the effects due to a change in the percentage of women of childbearing age in the population. A more careful economic analysis should take this effect into account. This effect is small as compared with the economic effects mentioned above because the percentage of women of childbearing age in the Chinese population did not change substantially in the periods mentioned.)

Economic factors alone would reduce the birth rate from 1980 to 1998. When economic development and urbanization occur, women can work and raising children will be costly in terms of the foregone earnings of the mother. In addition, the cost of having children is high in cities as compared with farm areas, in terms of food, housing, schooling and the impossibility to use them as workers as in farm families. The high cost discourages people living in cities to have children, as the experience of many countries including China has conclusively demonstrated.

In summary, when we consider the effects of having more children, we should consider not only the cost of raising them, but also the happiness they bring to the parents today as well as the benefits they will provide to the parents and to the society in the future. Even if we consider only the cost for children today, China's output growth rate since 1980 has been high enough to support a natural growth of population without the intervention of a one-child family policy. In addition, economic factors will naturally reduce the birth rate as has been experienced in other countries in the process of economic development and demonstrated by China's own development experience.

A Large Population Has Its Advantages

I hope to have convinced the reader that there is no need for China to control the increase of its population. In fact there are two advantages for a country to have a large population.

More People Means More Power and Influence

The first advantage is well recognized. Having a large population makes a country more important. It attracts the world's attention and increases China's influence in the world. The concept of democracy is based on "one person one vote." If the world had a democratic government, China would have more votes than any other nation. If all men are created equal, the populous China has to count more. Although the world does not have a democratic government, the large number of Chinese does count in terms of the economic power and political influence of the country. The large economic output produced by the abundance of high-quality human capital in China provides the basis of China's exports to all over the world and of China's large domestic market for foreign investors and exporters. China has a strong influence in the deliberations of the United Nations.

Favorable Scale Effects of a Very Large Population

The other advantage is the scale effect. A large group of people may be able to create more than they would if they were divided into smaller groups. One company of 10,000 persons may generate more profits than two companies of 5,000 persons each. When the population is larger, it is easier to find extremely talented people. The strength of a country is often measured by the quality of its best, and not by the average quality of all people. The best people provide leadership in all the important aspects of a country's economic and social life, in establishing and directing the most advanced industrial, financial, educational and research institutions, in providing innovations for these institutions and in conducting social and public affairs. The United States is strong partly because of people like Albert Einstein and Henry Ford. China can do very well because the most talented can be selected from such a large population pool.

A second aspect of the scale effect is that a large population provides a large market. China's economy can grow by the very large demand from its own large population. Potential innovators in China have a better incentive to invent because a new product can generate more revenue if it is sold to satisfy a large market. When I point out the above advantages of having a large population, I do not imply that a country needs a large population in order to be rich but only that having a large population confer the advantages as described. Certainly, a country with a small population can also be rich if the people are talented and the economic institutions are good.

To conclude, I suggest that the very large population of China presents no problem. Instead, it confers some advantages to China in terms of its importance in the world arena and the favorable scale effects.

Education, Science and Technology

To describe China's education system I will begin with its historical background, from imperial China to the Republic of China and then to the early years of the People's Republic of China. Concerning the current system, I will discuss educational institutions at different levels, with emphases on higher education, the role of government and non government educational institutions, the characteristics of China's universities, their students, and the prospects for improvement. I will also discuss family education briefly. Then I will turn to science, and to technology. The Chinese have tried very hard to promote education, science and technology for the purpose of modernizing their country and for economic development. They have succeeded to a large extent, and further improvement can be expected in the future.

Historical Background of Formal Educational Institutions

It is useful to provide some historical background of China's formal educational systems before discussing its current state. Beginning with the Han dynasty, China had a civil service examination system to select government officials. This system was modified and perfected in the Tang and subsequent dynasties. In the Qing period, there were different levels of examinations, analogous to the present-day primary, secondary and university levels. To advance in society, the main channel was to pass the examinations at various levels. Government officials were accorded the highest status in society, and merchants a low status. In addition, money and wealth came with government positions. Families dreamed of their children passing these examinations at the highest level possible. Education therefore became very important in Chinese thinking. This partly explains why Chinese-American parents drive their children to study so hard. Many of them still do not appreciate the fact that in the United States, one can be successful in all professions, including and especially in acting and in sports. The Chinese thought studying was the main way to obtain good government positions. The subject covered in the examination was mainly classics, especially Confucian classics.

Historians have commented that the imperial governments adopted the Confucian teaching in order to preserve social order and their political power. Some are critical of the ideas of Confucianism, which we have briefly touched upon in Chapter 1 while discussing the Han dynasty. One can point out the merits of the imperial examination system based on Confucianism. By studying the work of Confucius a government official learned kindness, honesty and loyalty to the emperor, to other officials and to friends. He was taught ways to improve his knowledge by observing and studying the world around him and to learning from other people. Such preparation can be considered useful for the official. At least it worked for hundreds of years. Under this examination system, many children studied at home, with tutors hired by the family. Sometimes, one tutor taught a group of children from different families in the neighborhood. The people having passed the examination at the highest level were placed in an academy from which the government appointed officials when needed.

The system began to break down in the beginning of the 20th century. After the defeat by the British in the Opium War of 1840–2, and defeats by other countries that followed until the turn of that century, the imperial government of the Qing dynasty realized that the education system had to be changed to modernize China. Peking University was established in 1896 by the Qing government. In terms of the organization of the university and the subjects taught, Peking University adopted features from the modern university system. Educational institutions at lower level began to change too. Primary and secondary schools began to appear; each requires six years of education like the United States. American missionaries and educators, as well as those from other countries including France, the United Kingdom, and Germany in particular, established high schools and universities in China. I attended Lingnan University and its affiliated primary and middle schools in Hong Kong, Macao and Guangzhou from the second grade to the freshman year. Lingnan was established by American missionaries in Guangzhou in 1888. It was closed in 1952 by the government of the People's Republic of China, and later reopened as Lingnan (University) College of Zhongshan University at the previous campus. I serve as its Honorary President and a member of its Board of Trustees.

Not only did education institutions change their forms, so did the subjects taught. In both respects, China was modernized. During the transitional period in the beginning of the 20th century, traditional education, provided by tutors at home or in local schools, continued to exist. Families could choose between these two kinds of schools for their children. Later, even those who sent their children to modern primary schools would hire a tutor to teach them Confucian classics. In the modern schools, Confucian classics was not studied in the same way and to the same extent as before, although the ideas and teachings of Confucius and other major ancient philosophers were still presented to the students in textbooks. When I attended primary school in Hong Kong and middle school in Macao in the 1930s and1940s, a family tutor was hired to teach me classics. It included essays of well-known scholar-officials and writers other than the great philosophers.

By the 1930s China's modern school system resembled the American system in many respects. The 6–6–4 years of attendance required at the three levels were American. The subjects taught were similar to the subjects taught in American schools. Of course, Chinese language and history replaced the American language and history. Mathematics and science were taught similarly. The level of mathematics and science in Chinese high schools was higher than in the United States. Today, this is said to be true for China and other Asian countries and many European countries. American educators are reexamining the US high school and elementary school curricula. I have not studied this closely, and am not prepared to conclude that making the subjects taught in schools more difficult for children and young teenagers in the United States is necessarily a good thing. There were also schools in China following the French or German model, but as a broad generalization the Chinese educational institutions resembled those of the United States in form and in the subjects taught.

This generalization is partly due to the rule of the Nationalist government. Chiang Kai-shek was its leader. Madame Chiang graduated from Wellesley College. The Chinese and American governments were friendly to each other. Besides, there was already a large American influence through the missionaries, and through the many leading Chinese scholars who had studied in the United States. Some of these scholars had received financial support from the US government, which decided to support Chinese students to study in the US by using the war indemnity from China after China lost the war following the Boxer Rebellion in 1900. My two older brothers came to the US to study in the late 1930s since US universities had similar curricula but were better in quality.

In China before 1949, public and private educational institutions coexisted. At the lower levels the government in each location of each province, under the direction of the national government, adhered to the policy of providing public education to Chinese children. The prevalence and quality of lower-level education provided by public schools varied from location to location, depending partly on its income level. Private schools were also available. Some were better than public schools and collected higher tuition fees. In Guangzhou in the 1930s and 1940s, the best high schools were private schools. At least these schools were considered by the citizens to be better. The well to do people sent their children to these schools when they could have sent them to public schools. Less well to do parents would also send their children to these private schools if they were given scholarships to equalize the costs of both types of schools. At the college level, the government had established some of the best universities in the country. Although there were comparable private universities, most people thought that the best five national universities, including Peking, Tsinghua, Jiaotong, Nankai and perhaps Nanking, were academically stronger than the best five private universities, although one or two private universities such as Yanjing was considered as good. Overall, the Chinese schools at all levels in the 1930s and 1940s were quite good, given the fact that modern education was a fairly recent development.

Education in the People's Republic of China

After the establishment of PRC, the education system can be discussed in terms of two periods, pre- and post-1978. During the first period, and soon after the government decided to adopt the Soviet type of economic planning in the early 1950s, the system of higher education was modeled after the Soviet Union along with economic planning. The government controlled all educational institutions. All private universities were closed. Liberal education ceased to exist. Education served mainly the purpose of economic development. For this purpose it was believed that a university student should concentrate on one subject, rather than receiving a general liberal education, and that each university should specialize too. Former universities, public and private, were reconstituted.

One university was broken up into several more specialized institutions. For example, the school of arts and sciences, the medical school, the engineering school, and the school of agriculture from previous universities were separated and became colleges on their own. Each ministry responsible for the production and distribution of one major product had under its control colleges to train people to work in a specialized area. The People's Bank administered a graduate school to train staff for the Bank and its branches in different provinces. The People's University was established to train people to work in the government.

At lower levels during the pre-reform period, the government also controlled all educational activities. Such control served two purposes. First, the government was welfare minded. It wanted to raise the level of education for the people. It did succeed in raising the literacy rate among population 15 years of age from a very low level in 1952 to 82 percent in 1978. Second, the government wanted to inculcate certain ideas of nationalism and communism to the children. No private schools were allowed. To see the expansion in education the reader may refer to Table 5.1 on school enrollment at different educational levels. The enrollment figures have not been adjusted for the increase in population in the corresponding school age.

The education system was greatly interrupted during the Cultural Revolution of 1966–76. During that period intellectuals

Table 5.1   Student enrollment by level of school, 1949 to 1981[a]

(10,000 Persons)

| Year | Total | Institutions of Higher Learning | Secondary Schools[b] | | Primary Schools |
			Secondary Specialized Schools	Regular Secondary Schools	
1949	2,577.6	11.7	22.9	103.9	2,439.1
1950	3,062.7	13.7	25.7	130.5	2,892.4
1951	4,527.1	15.3	38.3	156.8	4,315.4
1952	5,443.6	19.1	63.6	249.0	5,110.0
1953	5,550.5	21.2	66.8	293.3	5,166.4

Table 5.1 (*Continued*)

(10,000 Persons)

Year	Total	Institutions of Higher Learning	Secondary Schools[b] Secondary Specialized Schools	Regular Secondary Schools	Primary Schools
1954	5,571.7	25.3	60.8	358.7	5,121.8
1955	5,788.7	28.8	53.7	390.0	5,312.6
1956	6,987.8	40.3	81.2	516.5	6,346.6
1957	7,180.5	44.1	77.8	628.1	6,428.3
1958	9,906.1	66.0	147.0	852.0	8,640.3
1959	10,489.4	81.2	149.5	917.8	9,117.9
1960	10,962.6	96.2	221.6	1,026.0	9,379.1
1961	8,707.7	94.7	120.3	851.8	7,578.6
1962	7,840.4	83.0	53.5	752.8	6,923.9
1963	8,070.1	75.0	45.2	761.6	7,157.5
1964	10,382.5	68.5	53.1	854.1	9,294.5
1965	13,120.1	67.4	54.7	933.8	11,620.9
1966	11,691.9	53.4	47.0	1,249.8	10,341.7
1967	11,539.7	40.9	30.8	1,223.7	10,244.3
1968	11,467.3	25.9	12.8	1,392.3	10,036.3
1969	12,103.0	10.9	3.8	2,021.5	10,066.8
1970	13,181.1	4.8	6.4	2,641.9	10,528.0
1971	14,368.9	8.3	21.8	3,127.6	11,211.2
1972	16,185.3	19.4	34.2	3,582.5	12,549.2
1973	17,096.5	31.4	48.2	3,446.5	13,570.4
1974	18,238.1	43.0	63.4	3,650.3	14,481.4
1975	19,681.0	50.1	70.7	4,466.1	15,094.1
1976	20,967.5	56.5	69.0	5,836.5	15,005.5
1977	21,528.9	62.5	68.9	6,779.9	14,617.6
1978	21,346.8	85.6	88.9	6,548.3	14,624.0
1979	20,789.8	102.0	119.9	5,905.0	14,662.9
1980	20,419.2	114.4	124.3	5,508.1	14,627.0
1981	19,475.3	127.9	106.9	4,859.6	14,332.8

[a]Excludes spare-time schools.
[b]Excludes workers' training schools.
Source: *Statistical Yearbook of China*, 1981, p. 451.

were badly mistreated. Many universities were closed. In the years 1970 and 1971, student enrollment in institutions of higher learning was drastically reduced, as shown in Table 5.1.

Education Reform After 1978

After 1978 Deng Xiaoping initiated economic reform towards a market-oriented economy. Education was an important part of this reform process. University enrollment showed a very rapid increase in years 1978 to 1981, as shown in Table 5.1. The system for higher education was changed. The main direction was to abandon the Soviet-style education system introduced in the 1950s in favor of a more American-like system of the 1940 for higher education. For education at all levels, the government has allowed "citizen-operated" schools to develop and flourish side by side with the schools administered by the government at all levels.

The gradual change experienced in education reform, as in economic reform, has taken two and a half decades and is still incomplete, but in both cases we can see what has been accomplished. Higher education has become less specialized, with universities formed by merging previously separated colleges of medicine, engineering and agriculture and so forth. While the Ministry of Education in Beijing still controls some 30 major universities, the remaining state universities are under the control of the governments of provinces, cities and townships. The curricula, economics in particular, have changed to suit the working of a market economy.

In regard to the teaching of economics, Marxian economics is still taught although the interest in it has declined. Courses to explain the functioning of the macro- and micro-economy, on accounting, statistics, international trade, public finance, economic development, money and banking, econometrics and mathematical economics that are taught in American universities are being developed and have attracted a large number of students. In 1988, the Ministry of Education (then the State Education Commission) adopted a number of "core courses" including most of the courses listed above and decreed their adoption as required courses in the economics curriculum. When we read a university bulletin we find such courses, but we should not conclude that the quality of education for an average economics major in China is as high as that of a good American university. A government decision to require such courses does not guarantee the quality of the teaching. China needs qualified teachers in economics and other social science and humanity subjects. Only the mathematics courses taught to economics majors are of good quality, comparable to the best in the United States. Economics courses that require the use of mathematics are not well taught because most instructors do not yet master the subject. Reform in economics education has been completed in form to a large extent but not in substance.

The quality of university education in natural sciences, mathematics and engineering is quite good in China. The top schools have achieved world standards. Teaching and research in these subjects have not been affected by political ideology in the same way as subjects in social sciences have. On the contrary, the Chinese government has encouraged research in natural science and engineering as an important aspect of its modernization effort, as we will discuss later.

Quality of University Faculties

We first turn to the limited number of qualified faculty members. The number of qualified professors in mathematics, science and engineering are adequate for the top universities but not sufficient for the country as a whole. The numbers are more limited in social sciences. In humanities, Chinese universities are strong when the subject is closely related to Chinese culture. The government of the PRC emphasized higher education in mathematics, natural science and engineering as these fields have been recognized to be useful for China's modernization. Scholars in these fields have been treated as national heroes for their accomplishments, as model workers have been similarly treated for theirs. On the opposite extreme, social sciences as studied in the West were considered useless, if not ideologically incorrect. Fields like economics and sociology as we know in the United States ceased to exist in Chinese universities from the middle 1950s to 1980. The Chinese universities have a lot to catch up in these fields, but for a country as large as China, playing catch-up is a very time consuming process. It takes about 15 years just to train one scholar, with four years in college, about five years for a PhD degree and about six more years to become a mature scholar. Before this training can take place, an academic institution needs a group of such scholars and some more advanced ones in residence. In the middle of 1980s when China's Ministry of Education decided to introduce modern economics as a subject in the universities, there were only a handful of Chinese scholars trained in this subject.

To modernize the teaching of economics, the necessary first step was to find a group of qualified foreign professors to start training Chinese first-year graduate students. But the trained students could not advance further in China because there were no departments with sufficient qualified scholars who could continue to train them after the visiting professors left. It was also necessary to send Chinese students abroad to get their PhDs and wait for them to return to China. The first group would take at least five years to get their PhDs and perhaps two to three more years to become intellectually mature enough to return to China to teach, if they should decide to return. Since many economics PhDs from China found attractive job opportunities in the United States and elsewhere, most did not return. However the number of returning scholars, including those who have been to Hong Kong, has been increasing rapidly since the late 1990s, and the number returning to the Mainland has also increased since about 2000. These scholars form a nucleus to promote economics education in China. The

"If you want to pass this course, you must pass the Chow Test ..."
Passing Chow Test, Professor Gregeory Chow Lecturing at Shandong

(Professor Harvey Lam of Princeton provided the humorous comment based on the author's research interest.)

"To achieve market economy, you must understand the Lagrange Multiplier ..."
Understanding Lagrange Multiplier, Professor Gregeory Chow Lecturing at Shandong

(Professor Harvey Lam of Princeton provided the humorous comment based on the author's research interest.)

scholars remaining in the United States, Canada and other developed countries are also returning to lecture and offer consultation during short-term visits. As a result, although economics education in the entire country still lags behind the most advanced countries, it is improving rapidly through the efforts of the Chinese scholars who have studied abroad, and the teaching and research in a few leading institutions are up to international standards.

In humanities China has qualified scholars in fields related to China's culture. Chinese universities are excellent in Chinese literature. I believe they are also good in Chinese history. This last statement is somewhat controversial depending on one's viewpoint. A Chinese historian may know more about Chinese history than a history professor in the United States who has spent less time in studying Chinese classics and Chinese history through the 24 great history books, each for one dynasty or historical period. Yet the American professor is trained to interpret history with a broader perspective (perhaps this is also what the Chinese historian would fend for himself), to relate history to modern social sciences, and to do research using a variety of historical material using "scientific method." Chinese history books have conflicting accounts of the same events. Perhaps modern historical method can help resolve the conflict by appealing to evidence other than written material.

It seems fair to say that both traditional Chinese historical studies and modern studies of Chinese history have their merits. Contemporary historians in China are trained in both in varying degrees. In addition to studying history as a modern historian, they would appreciate the wisdom in Chinese classics as illustrated by quotations from the great historian Sima Qian in Chapter 1. As compared with most Western scholars, they are likely to have better reading skills for classical Chinese material. They may have a deeper "understanding" (as in understanding the meaning of a poem and not necessarily in scientific terms) of the Chinese cultural background in providing a suitable context for the study of history. Traditional Chinese scholarship has its own value in the study of

Chinese art, literature, philosophy, religion and other fields of humanities. It might even be valuable for the study of humanities in general from a comparative perspective. Its value will lend support to the conclusion that while China's universities are weak in the social sciences, they are strong in humanities related to the Chinese culture.

Institutional Characteristics of China's Universities

We next consider the institutional characteristics of China's universities. First in terms of organization a Chinese university is similar to an American university. It is headed by a president, divided into schools or colleges that are headed by deans, and further divided into departments headed by chairpersons. By and large the faculty plays a more important role in the selection of the university president. At the major universities under the direct supervision of the Ministry of Education in Beijing, the Ministry has the right to appoint and remove a president. In practice, however, the Ministry sends a committee to visit the university to talk to faculty members and to administer a straw poll among the faculty members on the candidates for the presidency. The person receiving more faculty votes will be appointed as a rule. By contrast, in Princeton University the Board of Trustees appoints the president, and no faculty votes are taken. Faculty voice is heard in a search committee that makes recommendations to the Board, together with recommendations from other sources, but the Board has final say and the voice of the faculty has only limited influence.

Second, Chinese universities are in general overstaffed. In a good American university, one faculty serves about 11 students. (The ratio of staff to faculty in American universities was increasing in the last three decades of the 20th century, partly because of the need to perform tasks specified by the Federal government.) In China in the 1980s, the ratio of students to faculty and staff was close to one. One employee of the university was required to serve one student.

127

This was the result of the economic planning system. The supporting staff working in hospitals and other service facilities affiliated with a university was counted in the above ratio. Graduates did not go out to look for jobs, and tended to remain in their own universities to become a member of the teaching staff. There was no need for the university administration to reduce the number of its staff. As a result universities were overstaffed, as were state enterprises, but the number of qualified teachers can still be insufficient.

Third, in terms of freedom of movement of faculty members, American professors are completely free to change jobs. It is still harder for a Chinese professor to move to another university than for an American professor, but his freedom has greatly increased. The lack of freedom to move was one aspect of the previous planned economy. Jobs were assigned by a labor bureau to people to work in factories and educational institutions and not determined by mutual agreement between employers and employees who searched for jobs. Urban residents of all professions also needed a residency permit to obtain the necessary rationed food items, and could not move to another city without a residency permit. As the market economy resumes operation, people no longer rely on a residency permit to get the necessities of life, as they are now available in the market place. It is, thus, not uncommon nowadays to have professors move from one university to another.

Fourth, in terms of academic freedom, the Chinese universities are reasonably good. By and large professors are free to do their research, to publish what they write and to teach what they think the students should learn. On freedom of speech, students and faculty members can say what they want, but they would be restrained if they were to advocate the overthrow of the government. It is all right to criticize the government on its policies, unlike the days in the 1950s when intellectuals were mistreated for criticizing certain government policies. In 1957,

Mao started a "Hundred Flowers Campaign" to encourage intellectuals to speak out. Some fell into his trap. When they did speak out he punished them. Such wrongdoings are not repeated today. In private gatherings among students or faculty members, one hears conversations as free as any other American universities. The reason why a high degree of freedom exists is that the government no longer feels threatened by such conversations. Furthermore, even if some government bureaucrats may not like it, they no longer have the apparatus to control it and no one who overheard an objectionable conversation has any incentive to report it to the government either. The potential informant does not know to whom he should report and even if he does, he gains nothing by reporting it and may lose friendship and become unpopular.

Fifth, concerning salaries of academia, compensations for university faculty members have increased rapidly in recent years and continue to increase. In 2002, the regular salary of a full professor is about 2,000 *yuan* a month. Most have supplementary income, from additional teaching at the home university or elsewhere, making a total monthly income of around 3,000 *yuan*. Although the exchange rate is 8.3 *yuan* for a dollar, in terms of purchasing power, such salary is equivalent to about 1,500 US dollars per month. Housing is subsidized. Home cooking with material worth one *yuan* may be as good as home cooking using one dollar in the United States if the ingredients are purchased in markets with a much lower cost of distribution than in the supermarkets in the US. A Chinese professor with the above income seems to live well. He does not have a car, but there is little need for it when he lives in university housing and has convenient public transportation.

In order to build a few world-class universities, Chinese leaders in the late 1990s decided to allocate a large sum in terms of billions of US dollars to the top few Chinese universities including Peking University and Tsinghua University. Although these universities in China cannot be expected to match Harvard or MIT in the near future, the effort did have an important impact on raising the standards of the top universities. Because the group of professors in China remained the same after the policy was introduced, a result of spending this amount of money was to raise the salaries of those moving to the very few selected universities and to exert upward pressure on the faculty salaries of the remaining universities. Chinese universities have also obtained financial support from provincial and city governments, institutions and individuals.

In the late 1990s Mr. Li Ka Shing from Hong Kong contributed 200 professorships to China, each paying 100,000 *yuan* annually. At the time the annual salary of an ordinary professor was about 12,000 *yuan*. In 2001 Tsinghua University received 16 professorships from certain financial institutions each paying one million *yuan* per year. These professorships are mainly used to invite professors from the United States, especially those originally from China, to teach for up to one year, with the salary prorated. The above annual salary, converted to US dollars, is not considered high for a visiting professor. These special professorships are helping to improve the quality of education in Tsinghua University. In general, the salaries of faculty in China are low by international standards, making it difficult for the universities to attract scholars from abroad. However, a few universities are paying internationally competitive salaries in total compensation, in terms of matching purchasing power, to attract Chinese graduates from abroad to return to teach. More are indeed returning to help improve the Chinese universities.

Non-Government Educational Institutions

Educational institutions at all levels continued to improve not only through the efforts of the central, provincial, and local governments but also by the efforts from the non-government sectors. "Citizen-operated" or privately financed schools at all levels have become widespread because there is large demand for them as the Chinese people have become richer and because the schools can be profitable. In the late 1980s I visited a primary school near Guangzhou that was established privately. The parents had to pay 100,000 *yuan*, worth about US$30,000 at the time, at the beginning of the first year for a six-year primary school education for one child. The investors of this school used the money to build a building on a piece of land leased from the town government at a low rent to encourage education. The school was said to be profitable. It was very good in terms of the quality of the teachers and the orderly behavior of the students. Often such schools were established formally by, or in the name of, an association. Associations of all forms sprang up rapidly in China after the economic reform started. If a state-owned enterprise could, and was supposed to, run a school for the children of its workers, why could a hospital not run a school for the public? Why could an association of artists in Shanghai not run a school also? Associations are accorded some legal status which a private individual may not possess. They have already invested certain fixed costs in the right to use land or a building, the establishment of some legal status, the personal connections of its management and staff and the public recognition of the organization that can be exploited to start a school or another kind of business.

Non-government schools have grown rapidly not only because they are economically viable, but also because many overseas Chinese are willing to support them. Chinese beyond the Chinese mainland have poured money to support all kinds of education in China. Both financial resources and knowledge on administering educational institutions were supplied to China for its benefit, as in the case of foreign investment, except that the former is non-profit. An investor contributes both her time and money to improve education in China. Observers have pointed out that the Chinese education system is deficient partly because the government spends too little on education. They would cite statistics on the amount of government expenditure expressed as a percent of GDP to support this claim. In 1995, public expenditure on education was only 2.5 percent of GDP in China, as compared with 5.4 percent in the United States and 5.2 percent as the world average. These statistics have not taken into account the non-public expenditures, contributions by overseas Chinese and other friends, and the spending by the parents to pay tuition in "citizen-operated" schools. Foreign contributions to education in certain towns, counties and villages are substantial, including in particular some towns and villages near Hong Kong.

The importance of privately financed education in China and some other countries has been documented in a report *Financing Education — Investments and Returns,* published in 2002 by the United Nations Educational, Scientific and Cultural Organization (UNESCO) and the Organization for Economic Cooperation and Development (OECD), which focuses on 16 emerging economies. Funds from a wide range of private sources, including individuals and households, contribute much more to education in these countries than in the OECD member states. In Chile, China and Paraguay, for example, more than 40 percent of the total amount spent on education comes from such private sources. The OECD average is 12 percent. There has been a rapid development of private education services in these countries, from wholly private, independent institutions to schools that have been subcontracted by governments to non-governmental organizations. In China and Zimbabwe, government-subsidized, community-managed schools are said by the above report to be the backbone of the education system. In the US, only a small fraction of expenditures on K-12 schools is private.

Family Education and Self Education

One important component of education in China is family education. Family education is important for other countries as well. It affects one's general knowledge and skill, working habits, attitude toward life, and the way one learns after growing up. In China it is based upon the skills, knowledge and attitudes that have been inherited and improved upon from generation to generation. While the Chinese farmers have learned farming from their parents and grandparents, the Chinese workers have picked up their skills from other workers and artisans at least from the Shang dynasty onwards. The Shang dynasty was marked by people who already knew how to make the beautiful bronze vessels that we see in art museums. A person who has received a good family education may be better off than another person with poor family education but has acquired a college degree. The first person can be better motivated, has better working habits than a below-average college graduate, and may have better people skill than the college graduate. China's family education has benefited from the Confucian cultural traditions of hard work, loyalty and honesty. There is also the negative side of Confucianism that goes with it, including perhaps the lack of creativity and originality. The Chinese family is a close-knit unit. Children are influenced by their parents to a large extent. Many children depend on family education as a very important part of their education.

To form a comprehensive picture of education in China, one must also include self education. When I gave a seminar on China's economic transformation in an Ivy League university, an informed person in the audience asked why China could achieve such a high rate of economic progress when its education system was so poorly financed. He cited the small amount of public expenditure on education as a percent of GDP as I have reported earlier in this chapter. The first part of my reply was that the expenditures on education provided by privately financed schools were widespread. The tuitions are paid by the parents; some of the schools are partly financed by overseas Chinese as discussed previously. The second part of my answer was about family education. The statistics on expenditures on education reflect neither components of the Chinese education system mentioned above. After the seminar, my good friend who hosted and chaired the seminar told me a very important point that I had missed. He said that he had visited China recently, and needed a guide who could speak English. He found one who spoke perfect English. He asked how the guide had learned English so well. The reply was, "I learned it myself." Perhaps some credit should be given to the family education and the influence of Chinese culture that motivated the guide. It is also possible that the guide had a special talent in learning a foreign language.

Distinguished Features of Chinese Students

What are the distinguishing features of students in China? First the Chinese students by and large tend to take their studies seriously. There are at least two reasons for this. One is the Confucian cultural tradition imbedded in the imperial examination system. The second is the current economic opportunities available to educated people in China. Students study hard as by doing so they will receive a better training and make a better living in the future. Tourists have often found Chinese on a university campus or in other public places reading a book in English, because knowledge of English is sellable.

Second, cultural tradition has also caused many Chinese students to be better in memorizing than in understanding, and better in understanding than in developing their own original ideas. Learning is achieved by memory to a large extent. To remember something is one aspect of the learning process. To understand is another aspect. In order to increase knowledge, it is necessary to create one's own ideas. The Chinese is strongest in the first and weaker in the third, as many Chinese educators recognize. They are trying to find ways to improve the creativity and originality of Chinese students. We have found Chinese graduate students in the United States doing very well in passing PhD qualifying examinations, but do not do as well in writing an original thesis. Of course there are plenty of very outstanding PhD theses written by students from China. These bright students have learned to become original in their thinking in spite of the lack of such training in most educational institutions in China. Generally speaking, strength in the first two characteristics, coupled with high energy and motivation as well as good studying habits, enables the Chinese students to do well. It is hoped that the small number of creative people will teach others to be creative in China in the course of time.

Science

Ever since the Chinese wanted to modernize their country in order to save China from imperial domination, they have considered science to be important. They realize that scientific knowledge can be translated into a strong military for defense and modernization of the economy. In the May 4 Movement of 1921, patriotic Chinese youth discussed two main ideas for the modernization of China — science and democracy. These were what the modernized Western imperial powers had and China lacked. Under the government of the Republic of China the Chinese intellectuals emphasized science more than other fields of study. Parents and teachers encouraged the young students to take up science, at the expense of other subjects. When I came to the United States as a student, I found that a vast majority of students from China majored in science and engineering, a phenomenon still prevalent today. Only those who did not have the ability to study science and engineering chose to study other fields. The study of medicine, for example, was not highly regarded. Medical doctors in China were not well paid. There were plenty of them, In addition to Western medical doctors trained in medical schools, there were the traditional Chinese doctors who prescribe Chinese medicine. Their fees were low as compared with the MDs in the US because there were many of them competing in the market place. This runs contrary to the situation in the United States where the medical profession limited the training of new doctors partly to prevent competition.

The government of the People's Republic of China emphasizes the development of science and technology, together with the promotion of education, for the betterment of the country. These are the words of a Chinese government slogan which is still in effect today. In August 1999 under the sponsorship of the Chinese government, I co-chaired and helped organize an international conference in Beijing entitled, "science/technology and education for the betterment of the nation." The PRC government considers the promotion of science and technology to be very important in its effort to modernize the country and speed up economic development. Successful researchers are nationally recognized. For example, in February 2002, President Jiang Zemin personally conferred "national science and technology awards" to researchers who had achieved significant research results. The ceremony was broadcast on national TV and treated as a major event. The highest award carries five million *yuan,* in addition to the national recognition.

To promote research in science and technology, an Academy of Science has been established in Beijing, located in the northwestern part of the city. The best scientists in every important area useful for national development are gathered there. The scientists are well paid. Their working conditions are good. They have high social stature. There is also an Academy of Social Science in Beijing. Its research staff is much smaller, and the research budget per person is much lower, partly because the nature of its research does not require high-cost equipment but also because of less emphasis given by the government. The prestige and social status are lower. The emphasis on natural science as compared with social science is also indicated in the large budget of the National Natural Science Foundation that provides research grants to natural scientists. Its budget is about ten times the budget of the foundation supporting social science research. I serve as an advisor to the National Natural Science Foundation. In the late 1990s the government decided to encourage research in finance, partly because of the need to develop a modern financial market and a set of modern financial institutions. Research in finance using mathematical methods is classified under natural science, and is supported by the National Natural Science Foundation. The research grants are generous by Chinese standards. Using research in finance as an umbrella, other areas in economics including macroeconomics, money and banking, foreign trade and economic development are included for research support from the Foundation.

China has very good scientists. Their accomplishments are well recognized. China developed the atomic bomb early. It has advanced technology in aerospace and rockets. There are internationally recognized mathematicians, physicists, chemists, biologists and engineers in China. This is the result of hard work by Chinese scientists, government policies and a cultural tradition favoring scholarship. In the late 1990s a Chinese-American scientist Wen Ho Lee from Taiwan was accused of transmitting scientific secrets to enable China to improve its nuclear warheads. When I discussed this accusation with scientists in Princeton, several told me that the state of research by scientists in China was advanced enough to accomplish the result without the help of a foreign scientist, not to mention the fact that there was completely no evidence that Dr. Lee passed any classified information to the PRC. *The New York Times* later admitted to have reported the case incorrectly.

Technology

My impetus for writing this book came partly from a conversation with an executive of a high-tech firm on his way to Beijing on company business. He was much impressed by the high-tech explosion in China, and told me that the development was unparallel. This observation is consistent with the rapid development of semiconductor manufacturing in China. Taiwan Semiconductor Manufacturing Company (TSMC) is known to be a very successful company in Taiwan established in 1987. It is a leading company in the world for the production of semi-conductors and the largest independent semiconductor foundry, with a net worth that equals about one tenth of the total market value of all stocks traded in the Taiwan Stock Exchange. At the end of the 20th century it did not face much competition from Mainland China. However within a period of two to three years into the 21st century, TSMC realized that China was rapidly catching up. It started to move a part of its operations to China. Among the high-tech industries to experience rapid development, one can cite integrated circuits, the computer, telecommunications, biotech, and medicine.

Several factors have contributed to the explosion of high-tech industries in China. First, China offers a large supply of skilled labor of very high quality at low costs. This is the most important factor. Chinese scientists and engineers are excellent in supporting high-tech industries in research and development and in manufacturing. Second, the Chinese government encourages foreign investment in this area, providing favorable investment conditions such as low tax rates. After China joined the WTO in 2001, it became easier for foreign investors to enter China. They can now sell their products directly in Chinese domestic markets without going through Chinese agents. This cuts down their costs. The Chinese can learn very fast. After working in foreign invested enterprises, they learn the technology, the manufacturing procedures, the method of management, and marketing. Pretty soon, they can set up their own companies to compete. Third, on the demand side, not only is there a world market for high-tech products, the domestic market in China itself is large and rapidly growing. For example, both the demand for personal computers and the use of the internet are rapidly growing in China. Based on a forecast reported in Chow

(2002, p. 165), by the year 2015 there will be 21 computers per 100 households in China or about seven computers per hundred persons. This forecast is consistent with the report in *People's Daily*, July 22, 2003, that at the end of June 2003 China had 68 million internet users making up 5.3 percent of its population, second in number only to the United States. The number of computers is reported to be 38 percent of the Internet users, or 2.0 [5.3 (0.38)] percent of the population, but the rate of growth of the number of Internet users is about 26 percent per year in 2003. Compounding a 26 percent annual growth for five years would lead to an increase to a factor of 3.2, implying 3.2 times 2 or 6.4 percent of the Chinese population having a computer.

These are the reasons why high-tech industries have grown and will grow very rapidly. For the country as a whole China has the advantage of being a latecomer, and can learn from the developed countries. On that count, one can expect that it will be able to leapfrog and grow faster than the countries that had to spend time inventing the technology themselves. The introduction of high-tech consumer products, for example, can start from the latest, namely cell phones, without going through the stage of using a regular phone and is assisted by foreign investors.

To appreciate the high-tech explosion in China, consider the following foreign trade statistics reported on July 27, 2003 in the *People's Daily*. In the first half of 2003, China exported more than 44 billion US dollars worth of high-tech products, an increase of 54.6 percent from the same period in the year before. It accounts for 23 percent of the country's total export, with a growth rate 21 percentage point higher than that of total exports. Computer and telecommunications products contributed to 82.2 percent of the high-tech exports, growing by 61.5 percent year-on-year to 36.16 billion US dollars. Other products experiencing strong growth were mobile phones, electronic products and life science products. 19.55 billion worth of high-tech exports was produced in Guangdong province as the leading producer, followed by Jiangsu, Shanghai,

Tianjin, Fujian and Beijing. Foreign-funded enterprises exported 37.1 billion dollars of these products, accounting for over 84 percent of the total. One should not be surprised to see some of these products occupying an important place in the world market as the automobiles produced by Japanese firms.

In summary, higher education in China is in good condition in general, with strong instructions in physical science, engineering and certain areas of humanity but weaker in social science. The quality of education continues to improve, more rapidly for the top universities than for the nation as whole. The state of scientific research is quite advanced. Technology will improve rapidly. High-tech industries are experiencing a phenomenal growth. The dreams of several generations of Chinese to use science/technology and education for the modernization of their country have come true to a large extent and the future will be even brighter.

5

Government System and Performance

This chapter begins with a description of how the Chinese government is organized. It then discusses the performance of the government in terms of the freedom of the citizens, elections and political participation by the citizens, and the services provided to the citizens. I will also relate some personal experience in working with the Chinese government, and deal with the subjects of corruption and prospect of political reform.

How Is the Chinese Government Organized

China is ruled by the Communist Party. The Party has ultimate power and assumes leadership of the Chinese government.

The Communist Party was founded in 1921 by people with strong nationalistic ideals in order to lead China on its road to modernization. Some of the ideas of the founders, including the use of central economic planning instead of market economic institutions to achieve economic development, are no longer as attractive to many Chinese today as when the Party was founded. The party organization was modeled after the Soviet Communist Party, as was the organization of the Nationalist Party in many respects. Representatives of party organizations at low levels successively elect representatives at higher levels to produce members of the Central Committee of the Chinese Communist Party (numbered about 200 in the 16th Central Committee as of 2003). The members of the Central Committee elect members of the Political Bureau (of 24 persons as of 2003), who in turn select members of its Standing Committee (of nine persons in 2003). The last group has the highest political power in China. The Party Central Committee is headed by its General Secretary. The Chairman was the head until Chairman Mao Zedong's successor Hua Guofeng was replaced in 1978 by a General Secretary to signal the abolition of absolute power of the chairman.

To assume its leadership the Communist Party needs to exercise control over the government and other state organizations. The Chinese government is headed by a president. The executive branch of the government is the State Council. It is headed by a premier, assisted by several vice-premiers, and is composed of some 24 ministries and five commissions (having broader responsibilities or deemed more important than ministries). The legislative branch is headed by the National People's Congress. Members of this Congress are elected by members of provincial congresses, and the latter are successively elected from representatives of units below. By submitting a list of candidates for the high offices in the State Council and drafts of legislation for the approval of the People's Congress, the Central Committee of the Communist Party exercises its political leadership. Since most members of the People's Congress are members of the Communist Party, they tend to follow the party leadership in these matters, although dissent has occurred in recent years in the voting of candidates for offices and of proposed legislation.

In other state organizations such as state-owned enterprises and universities, party secretaries are installed to provide leadership alongside the heads of these organizations. In general the party secretary has more authority than the manager of an enterprise or the president of a university. In addition, the Party has established street committees in urban areas and village committees in rural areas to oversee the affairs of the people. Considered from a negative point of view, such party organizations infringe upon the privacy and freedom of the population. An example is the enforcement of birth-control policy with a Party representative checking the menstrual periods of the women in the district under his/her supervision. Considered from a positive point of view, the Party representative helps the people in the district in the same way that a Christian minister can help members of his congregation. For example, such a party organization can be useful to check the possible occurrence and spread of the SARS virus in China in the spring of 2003.

In addition to the central government, China has provincial and local governments. Formally speaking, the provincial governments are under the direction of the central government. This relationship is different from the relation between the state governments and the federal government in the United States. A candidate for governorship is submitted by the Central Committee of the Communist Party and approved by the People's Congress, as in the case of a high office of the State Council. The governor works under the direction of the central government. When there are important matters, such as decisions on economic reform, the governors are summoned to Beijing to receive directions from the central government. In practice, the degree of independence of the governors varies from province to province, partly according to historical tradition. For example, the southern province of Guangdong has been quite independent. To find a person who can rule Guangdong effectively, the central government has to select a local person or at least someone acceptable to the people of that province, and the person retains a fairly high degree of independence. The independence of Guangdong is also supported by the central government policy initiated by Deng Xiaoping in 1978 to allow it to go "one step ahead" in economic reform towards a market economy. The people of Guangdong have been traditionally more independent and subjected to less discipline, at least not by central authorities.

There are also five autonomous regions, Tibet, Guangxi, Ningxia, Xinjiang and Inner Mongolia. These are "provinces" granted more autonomy because they are inhabited by ethnic minority groups who desire self-rule. Hong Kong and Macao are special administrative regions (SAR) after they were returned to China by the British and the Portuguese governments respectively in 1997 and 1999. The municipalities of Beijing, Shanghai, Tianjin, and Chongqing are large cities placed under the direct control of the central government because of their importance. Governments of cities, counties and townships are under the provincial governments.

China has a Constitution adopted by the People's Congress on December 4, 1982. It consists of a Preamble and four chapters. The Preamble includes a statement, "The basic task of the nation in the years to come is to concentrate its effort in socialist modernization." In Chapter I, "General Principles," Article 2 states, "All power in the PRC belongs to the people. The organs through which the people exercise state power are the National People's Congress and the local people's congresses at different levels." Article 28 states, "The state maintains public order and suppresses treasonable and other counter-revolutionary activities; it penalizes actions that endanger public security and disrupt the socialist economy …" In Chapter II, "The Fundamental Rights and Duties of Citizens," Article 35 provides all citizens "freedom of speech, the press, assembly, association, procession and demonstration". Article 36 provides "freedom of religious belief." Chapter III, "The Structure of the State," specifies the composition and function of the National People's Congress, the President, the State Council, the Central Military Commission, the local people's congresses and governments, and the People's Court. Chapter IV has articles 136–139 on the national flag, national emblem and the capital respectively. There are amendments to the Constitution. By the amendment approved on April 12, 1988, "The State permits the private sector of the economy to exist and develop within the limits prescribed by law" in contrast with the original Article 11, which allowed only for "the individual economy of urban and working people." There are other amendments to the Constitution.

A major difference between the Chinese and American constitutions is that the former was approved by a congress under the leadership of the Communist Party. With this difference in mind one may be able to answer some puzzling questions about the Chinese constitution from an American perspective. How can the statement "All power in the PRC belongs to the people" in Article 2 be reconciled with the principle that the Communist Party assumes leadership of the government? A possible answer in the Chinese context, whether we agree with it or not, is that the Party is supposed to serve the people and help the people in electing their representatives in the People's Congress to exercise the power of the people. Legally speaking, the people exercise their power through their representatives in the People's Congress. In reality, the Communist Party guides and leads them in this process.

Another question concerns all the freedoms and human rights declared in Chapter II and the possible discrepancy between the stated freedoms and realities in China. Note Article 28 of Chapter I, which empowers the state to maintain public order, to suppress treasonable activities and to penalize actions that endanger public security. This power can be used to limit the freedom of the citizens. Perhaps many Chinese see less of a discrepancy in this regard as Americans do if they believe that the restriction of some of the freedoms is necessary for law and order and for the common good. The remaining discrepancies between the statements of the Constitution and actual practice can be attributed to the failure of the government to put the principles of the Constitution into practice. Many people in China, including members of the Communist Party, would agree that the Party and the government are imperfect in carrying out their responsibilities and need to be improved.

China's legislative system will be further discussed later in this chapter. Its judicial system has been discussed in Chapter 3 in connection with China's economic institutions

How Good Is the Chinese Government

How good is the Chinese government? I will answer this question in terms of three components of "political well-being" that the Chinese people can enjoy under the current government. The three components are: (1) freedom, (2) ability to participate in the selection of government officials, and (3) what the government has done and continues to do for the people. Instead of answering the question by simply examining whether the Chinese government is a "democratic government" according to some definition, it is more meaningful to consider these three components of political well-being for the following reasons. First, freedom is one of the most important ideals of democracy, but freedom can exist without a democratic government as it did in Hong Kong under the British colonial rule. Note that the inclusion of freedom as the first component is based on an American perspective because the Chinese have other ideals for their government, as we will discuss below. Second, the next important ideal of democracy is the ability to select government officials. It is better to consider the important democratic ideals than a set of procedures specified in a particular form of democracy subject to the tradition and practice of a particular country. The first two components of political well-being already include the most important institutional aspects of a democratic government from an American perspective. Third, given the same political system and form of democracy one government can be better than another because it does a better job to serve the people. Although the nature of the government system itself *may* be more important than the performance of particular government officials at a particular time, the latter can also be important. I emphasize the word "*may*" because a democracy can produce very bad leaders such as in the case of Adolf Hitler in Germany in the 1930s. Germany, and the world, might have been better off with a benevolent emperor.

The following discussion will emphasize the current political well-being in China rather than its past. Some of the mistakes of the Chinese government were discussed in Chapter 1. After economic reforms started in 1978, the Chinese Communist Party and its ideology began to change. So did the Chinese government, mostly to the better. The problems that the Communist Party faces are different from those in the early days of the PRC. Previously it was preoccupied with problems to destroy the old political and economic power base and to establish its own. Now the Party is in power and has learned from past mistakes. Its main desire is to be more constructive. Most of the past mistakes of the Party consisted of their destructive acts. Without dwelling on the mistakes of the Chinese government in the past, on which reading material abounds, I will make an assessment of the current government. Readers interested in learning about the disasters under the Communist rule in the past may search the Internet under "Great Leap Forward Movement" and "Cultural Revolution."

Freedom

Before discussing how much freedom the Chinese enjoy, I would like to note that the most desirable degree of freedom varies among countries and depends on the circumstances facing the citizens. More freedom is not necessarily desirable. Freedom has its negative side not only because one person's freedom may infringe upon another's, but also because individual freedom itself may not be the ultimate goal of a society. In Chinese culture, responsibility is valued more than freedom. Individualism has not generally been considered a virtue in China. This was so even before the establishment of the PRC in 1949. Collective welfare is considered as important as, if not more important than, individual freedom. This value system has resulted from China's historical tradition and has been affected by the environment in which the people lived.

The tragic event of September 11, 2001 in the United States demonstrates that the environment can affect the value system regarding the most desirable amount of freedom. Travelers are no longer free to board an airplane without being searched. Many Islamic American citizens are under surveillance. Human rights advocates complain that our freedom is reduced by government actions in response to 9/11. The new Department of Homeland Security reminds one of Article 28 of the Chinese Constitution that empowers the state to "penalize actions that endanger public security." In the Chinese society people consider law and order to be more important than freedom, although they resent inappropriate restrictions to individual freedom in the name of law and order. They also consider responsibility and tolerance as probably more important. The most desirable amount of individual freedom in China is probably less than in the United States. It is necessary to have social order before its citizens can have much freedom. Since there is a greater need to preserve social order in China, there is more limitation to freedom than in the United States.

Given their social environment, do the Chinese have sufficient freedom? They certainly did not in the 1960s and 1970s. At that time freedom was severely restricted. The Chinese people could not move freely from place to place, choose or change their jobs at will, leave the country freely, speak freely, form associations freely or assemble for religious worship. A leader in every city bloc or in every village carefully watched their activities. All the above restrictions to freedom have now been lifted.

Today, the Chinese people can travel freely both inside and outside the country. Many have come to the United States to study. They can choose and change their jobs fairly freely although many do not move because of the benefits of entitlements under the welfare system administered by state-owned enterprises. They can talk freely in private gatherings and even openly in professional meetings without fear of being prosecuted. For instance, a Chinese economics professor openly criticized the labor theory of value (a basic doctrine in Marxian economics) in a paper presented before a conference in Beijing in 1999. There is considerable freedom of the press as the non-government press has expanded rapidly in recent years and attracted a large readership. This includes daily or weekly newspapers, magazines and books. Opinions expressed therein are open and free, subject to only a minor degree of censorship. Censorship of foreign books is almost non-existent. Information available to the public is somewhat restricted because the government has control over TV and radio stations and even the Internet. However, the control is limited because the Chinese have access to short-wave radios and it is difficult to control the use of fax machines and the flow of information through the Internet. People residing near Hong Kong can get access to TV stations in Hong Kong, which are mainly private.

Most restrictions on freedom are based on Article 28 of the Constitution that empowers the state to suppress treasonable and counter-revolutionary activities, that is, activities against the state or the Communist Party. No one manages to advocate the overthrow of the Communist Party without endangering oneself. In China, there are political prisoners, who are considered to have acted against the government. The political dissidents include those who attempt to overthrow, or advocate the overthrow of, the government. Except for this restriction of political freedom, the Chinese people are free — free to speak, free to establish private enterprises, free to write and publish, free to assemble, free to worship and free to travel across different regions in China and to other countries.

If one compares the amount of freedom the Chinese people enjoy today with what existed before the establishment of the People's Republic of China in 1949, one may conclude that there was perhaps slightly more freedom before 1949. Under the rule of the Nationalist government, Chinese citizens could also be, and many were, executed for attempting to overthrow the Nationalist government. The situation under the Nationalists allowed more freedom because the government did not have much power to control many aspects of life of the Chinese people. The government did not have representatives on every street bloc or in each village to mind the affairs of the citizens. It did not control the number of children each family was allowed to have. There was a smaller bureaucracy to control the economic activities of the citizens. The press appeared to be somewhat freer, although advocating a Communist government was not allowed. On the positive side for the present Chinese society, the people today are richer and more educated so that they can travel and exercise their other freedoms. Although the current government has tried to control the press to a larger extent than did the government before 1949, it is more difficult to control information because of the modern technology of the fax machine and the Internet.

The one-child family policy introduced in 1980, relaxed to some extent in recent years, appears to me to be a serious violation of individual freedom and human rights in China. However, most Chinese citizens with whom I have discussed this matter support the government's one-child policy, as I have found when giving talks in China on the subject of population policy. Many of them think that the policy is necessary and desirable. I have discussed my opposing view in Chapter 4. Thus what I consider a restriction of freedom is not considered so by the majority of the Chinese people. In general, the Chinese may not complain about the lack of freedom as much as a Western observer may expect from his own perspective.

An issue related to freedom is human rights, as exemplified by the treatment of Tibet, *Falun Gong* and certain political dissidents. Here the views of the Chinese people may also differ from those of outside observers. On Tibet, most Chinese citizens (Han being the vast majority) side with the government in making sure that Tibet remains a part of China. Some Han Chinese believe that certain religious leaders in Tibet use the issue of religious freedom as a means to promote political independence. I may add that some Chinese citizens believe that China should have more religious freedom than what the government allows, while attendance at Christian church has been allowed to increase rapidly in recent years. On *Falun Gong* — whose practice involves meditation and breathing exercises and espouses mysticism that draws partly on traditional Chinese religion and philosophy — the vast majority of educated Chinese citizens, including those studying and working in the United States, believe that it is a cult and a menace to society. They tend to support the government in taking punitive actions. On the treatment of political dissidents, it depends on who the political dissidents are and the circumstances that turned them into one. The Chinese government is receptive to a constructive approach to this issue, such as the approach taken by John Kamm, a Princeton alumnus, in promoting human rights in China. Without criticizing the Chinese government, he was able to work with government officials to free a number of high-profile political prisoners in several occasions in the 1980s and the 1990s. Since 1998, China has cooperated with the Office of the United Nations High Commissioner for Human Rights to promote human rights as reported in the Commissioner's *Annual Report 2002*, pp. 87–89.

Most people in China do not consider human rights a major issue. Some intellectuals are resentful when foreigners criticize their country on this issue. They can easily find examples of violation of human rights at present or the recent past in the country of a critical foreigner. The Chinese are more concerned about how to improve their economic well-being under a stable government and tend to place more emphasis on law and order for the common good. In considering the conduct of their government, they think less about how much freedom they have than the performance of the government in providing them benefits, the third aspect of the government to be discussed below. Overall, the Chinese people can be quite satisfied with their government if political stability is provided for them to make money and if the government provides them with economic benefits. It would be useful for foreign observers interested in knowing how well the Chinese government performs to seek opinions from people living in China. Seeking the opinions of visiting students from China is also one way to find out, although the sample may not be representative of the many segments of the Chinese population.

Elections and Participation in Government Administration

On the second aspect of the Chinese government system, the process by which people elect their government representatives and officials, its importance is also dependent on social circumstances. The Chinese citizens may consider it to be less important than the third aspect, the provision of benefits by the government, to be discussed later.

The Chinese people can influence the affairs of the government in a number of ways. First, on the village level, there are now widespread direct elections. The citizens directly select officials to govern their own village. Such elections were not introduced by a policy of the central government from above. They were instituted from below when the organization of the Commune System collapsed in the early 1980s after collective farming was abolished. The civic affairs of the villages previously administered by the Commune System, such as the provision of security and the protection of public land, had to be attended to. Quite spontaneously, people in the villages wanted to elect officials to administer such affairs. The officials are nominated by the Party organization but individuals who are not Party members can seek nomination and many of them actually have been elected. On the village level, democracy in the Western definition prevails in China. The election is genuine because the villagers know whom they want to elect and the Party desires for its own good to get capable and popular people to take care of the affairs of these villages. However, direct election is generally not yet allowed for the selection of government officials on levels above the village.

Secondly, members of the legislatures at all levels are elected, though indirectly except for the lowest level. Direct election is practiced at the lowest level and members at higher levels are elected by the members from the level immediately below. The lowest level consists of villages in rural areas and districts in cities, where direct election takes place. Higher levels are townships, cities and provinces, and finally the National People's Congress. Some members of the People's Congress are not members of the Communist Party. Whether such indirect elections for legislators are better than direct elections at higher levels for China is a difficult question to answer. About 80 percent of the Chinese population live in rural areas and do not follow political affairs above the village level. Many of them are not interested in voting or not sufficiently informed to vote for candidates at the provincial or national levels.

Third, officials of the Communist Party are also indirectly elected by officials at the level immediately below. Ordinary citizens can participate in political affairs by first joining the Communist Party and taking part in the process of indirect elections. It is not easy to become a member of the Communist Party, which is made up of about eight percent of China's population. Membership requires certain qualifications and is considered an honor. China has a one-party system. There is a politically influential Chinese People's Consultative Conference composed of Party and non-Party members who can voice opinions about national affairs and government policies. The representatives of the Consultative Conference are influential citizens representing different ethnic groups, political parties and other social groups and are appointed by the Party. It meets simultaneously with the People's Congress to vote on recommendations for government policies, and the recommendations are taken seriously. It is not easy to discuss how good such a one-party system is in the Chinese context. It is taken for granted by most Chinese people. Since the late 1990s, Party membership has been extended to wider segments of the society including capitalists. The system can be improved by extending the opportunities for political participation further, including the nomination of non-Party members to government posts at all levels. The Communist Party considers the reform of the Chinese political system towards a more democratic system to be an important mission, as I will discuss at the end of this chapter.

Before ending this section on elections under a one-party system, I should call attention to the orderly succession of the leadership of the Communist Party. Some Western observers have the notion that there is a succession problem in China's political leadership. Yet all the historical successions under Communist rule have been peaceful and orderly. Before Mao died in September 1976 he designated Hua Guofeng to succeed him as Chairman of the Communist Party. Hua was Chairman for a short time until Deng Xiaoping became the leader. Deng was able to assume de facto leadership without being Chairman because the top party leaders supported him. The transition was peaceful. In fact Hua remained a member of the Central Committee of the Chinese Communist Party for two more decades. By 1978 Deng was in a position to initiate economic reforms. When Deng died in 1996, General Secretary Jiang Zemin took over leadership smoothly. In 2002, the position of General Secretary was transferred to Hu Jintao smoothly through election by the Central Committee. As we can see from the indirect election process within the Communist Party there is a due process of election for top leaders, including the General Secretary, step by step. To become a General Secretary, one has to get the support of the members of the Central Committee who elect members of the Political Bureau, and the latter in turn elect its standing committee. The members of the Central Committee are highly qualified people with experience in affairs of the government as they are so recognized and elected by lower-level Communist Party organizations. This accounts for the stability in the political structure of China.

What the Government Does for the People

The third aspect of China's government system, the political welfare provided by the government, is probably considered the most important of the three by Chinese citizens. The PRC government, in spite of its grave errors in the past, has done a great deal for the Chinese people. The first great accomplishment is the unification of China as a nation. After the revolution of 1911 when the government of the Qing dynasty was overthrown, China was politically divided. Military leaders of different provinces occupied their own territory to extract rents for themselves. There was no political stability. National unity was important to protect China from domination by foreign powers and to provide political stability and law and order. Law and order provided by the PRC government is important for economic and social progress.

As someone accustomed to law and order in the United States since 1948, it has taken me several visits to China to appreciate its importance. Several experiences impressed me. In 1982 while visiting Zhongshan University in Guangzhou, I needed to send a telegram and asked my host to stop the car by a post office to send it. He said he would send it for me. I insisted on doing it myself. When I entered the post office, I found that people did not line up in front of the service window and there was no way for me to get to the front to submit the draft of my telegram. I had to let my friend fight his way through and he succeeded in sending the telegram. I wished an officer had been there to guide people to line up. As a second experience, my wife Paula and I were provided a tour guide while visiting Confucius' Temple in Shandong province in 1985. As the guide was explaining the points of interest to us, people began to crowd in and surrounded the guide to the point that Paula and I were so far from him that we could not hear what he was saying. There was no order either. As a third example, I was traveling by car to visit the site of Yuan Ming Yuan, an old palace in Beijing destroyed by fire set by the British and French soldiers in 1858. As we approached the site, there was a roadblock set up illegally by local residents to collect tolls. Our driver had to pay the toll before he could drive through. Extraction of fees of all kinds by local residents from travelers passing through their territories was and is quite common in China. A strong government is needed to prevent this from happening.

The Chinese government realizes that law enforcement is a major problem because many Chinese are uninformed and not law-abiding. On June 29, 2003, the *People's Daily* reported a speech by Wu Bangguo, Chairman of the Standing Committee of the National People's Congress, as saying that "laws, rather than being regarded as simply words on paper, should be strictly respected and enforced," and "We must make greater efforts to promote knowledge of the legal system and of China's law in the long run." If the above personal encounters and official pronouncements are not sufficient to establish the importance of law and order, let me point to the infringement of intellectual property rights in the form of selling pirated CDs of computer software, music and movies in China.

Secondly the government has given pride to the Chinese people. After the Opium War of 1840–42, when China was defeated by the British, other wars followed and China had to sign unequal treaties to foreign powers, yielding territorial rights, rights to build railroads and rights to navigate in Chinese rivers, etc. A most important war was the Sino-Japanese War of 1900 when Japan took over Korea and Taiwan from China's sphere of influence. The Chinese people were humiliated. Their pride was hurt. It was the PRC government that finally restored their pride to a significant extent. For this they are willing to give up a small amount of personal freedom. They want a strong government to establish law and order inside China and to make themselves proud of being Chinese citizens. They have a strong sense of nationalism.

There are other services that they desire from the government. In any economy, the important functions of the government may include:

(1) the building of economic and social infrastructure,

(2) the provision of social welfare,

(3) the promotion of economic stability and growth, and

(4) the establishment or the fostering of selected enterprises or industries to compete in the international markets when the private sector does not have sufficient human or physical capital to do so.

The last function is termed industrial policy and has been questioned by economists who believe in the free market system, where private investors alone should decide on what new investment projects to undertake. However, in a developing economy, the capital market may be imperfect and not all the brains and all the necessary capital for investment are in the private sector.

On function (1) to build social and economic infrastructure, the track record of the Chinese government has been quite good. For the social infrastructure, since 1949, student enrollment has increased rapidly as shown in Table 5.1. According to Chinese official statistics in the section "Education" under "China At A Glance" of the home page of the website http://english. peopledaily.com.cn/ of the *People's Daily*, the illiteracy rate of the Chinese population decreased from about 80 percent in 1949 to 12 percent in 1997. Health care for the mass of Chinese people has improved. As a result of the improved health care and the more widespread use of boiled water for drinking, the death rate in China dropped dramatically as shown in Table 4.1, from 17 per year in one thousand persons in the population in 1952 to about 6.5 in year 2000. For the economic structure, during the period of economic planning, numerous factories were built; over 100,000 miles of railroads and highways were constructed and the postal and communications system was greatly expanded.

After 1978, the government successfully guided the reform from a planned to a market economy. This remarkable performance was made possible by the stability of the government system and the high degree of competence of government officials at different levels. The fact that very competent officials are selected to serve in the government is a credit to the government system which we have discussed earlier in this chapter. Through the system of indirect elections in both the Communist Party and the government, capable people have acquired responsible positions. Of course this is a generalization with many exceptions. Some people have acquired important government positions through personal connections.

On function (2), to provide social welfare, during the planning period up to 1978, the health care of people in the countryside was provided under the Commune System, while the urban population enjoyed health and retirement benefits, as well as job security and almost free housing provided by the state-owned enterprises. An efficient three-tier health care system, with barefoot doctors treating simple illnesses and local clinics and city hospitals in turn taking care of more difficult cases, covered almost the entire rural population. Clinics and hospitals associated with state-owned enterprises cared for the urban population. This welfare system ceased to function properly after economic reform and has been gradually replaced. Since the mid-1990, the Chinese government has attempted to set up a comprehensive social security system, under the central management of the labor and social security administration departments, with social insurance funds partly contributed by the central government. In 1997, a uniform basic old-age insurance system for enterprise employees was established, financed by 20 percent of the enterprise wage bill and eight percent of the employee's wage. Employees participating in this program increased from 86.71 million in late 1997 to 108.02 million at the end of 2001, with an average monthly basic pension per person of 556 *yuan*.

In 1998, a basic medical insurance system for urban employees was established, financed by six percent of the wage bill of employing units and two percent of the personal wages. By the end of 2001, 76.29 million employees had participated in basic insurance programs. In addition, free medical services and other forms of medicare systems covered over 100 million urban population. In 1999, an unemployment insurance system was introduced, financed by 2 percent of the wage bill paid by employers and 1 percent paid by employees. At present, it is difficult to evaluate China's social security system, since the entire system has not yet been completed and the observations of its functioning are limited. I can only report that the government has made a serious effort in this direction. Economists disagree on the most desirable form of social security, some suggesting a limited role for the government and a major role for private insurance and private savings.

On function (3) to promote economic stability and growth, since 1980, the government has tried to set up a modern macroeconomic control mechanism to replace central planning for this purpose. The record on stability up to the present has been reasonably good, with some exceptions. A major exception was the large credit expansion and increase in money supply for several years that led to the serious inflation in the fall of 1988. Inflation and government corruption were two important factors contributing to discontent among the population and demonstrations in Beijing, which ultimately led to the tragic event in Tiananmen Square on June 4, 1989. On economic growth, China's record has been excellent. The Chinese people deserve much credit for the rapid growth, but the government has guided the development of market institutions that provide them with sufficient economic incentives to work hard in generating the dynamic growth. Some of the important market institutions such as the household responsibility system in agriculture and the township and village enterprises were initiated from below, but the central government recognized their desirability and allowed them to develop.

Concerning function (4) to facilitate or direct investment in particular areas in the execution of an industrial policy, it is a Chinese tradition for government officials to initiate or guide investments in the private sector. In the late Qing dynasty, Chinese railroads were built partly through the financing by the Bank of Communications. This bank was established by a Qing minister named Liang Yansun. He had the foresight and ability to lead a group of private investors to set up this private bank. Liang served as its Chairman of the Board for many years, and the bank is still in operation in both Mainland China and Taiwan today. As a second example, Dr. K. T. Li, a trained physicist, who served in the government of the Republic of China in Taiwan in a number of important economic posts, played an important role in establishing the Kaohsiung Special Economic Zone to attract foreign investment and the Science Industrial Park in Hsinchu for the training of technical personnel and the development of high-tech industries. Both are regarded as highly successful undertakings. The experience of the former project has influenced the establishment of Special Economic Zones in China, including Shenzhen which borders Hong Kong. The latter contributed to the establishment of Taiwan Semiconductor Manufacturing Company, considered the most successful private enterprise in Taiwan in the 1990s, with its net worth equal to about one-tenth of the total market value of all stocks traded in the Taiwan Stock Exchange as of 2001.

The PRC government directed the development of heavy industry during the planning period. As economic reform started in the late 1970s, government officials realized the importance of light industry for the production of consumer goods and promoted it. In recent years, the government has tried to promote the development of high-tech industries by devoting its own resources in research and development as described in Chapter 5, and by directing state-owned enterprises and encouraging foreign investment to produce high-tech products. Although China has a market economy, the government plays an important role in directing the economic development of particular industries and particular regions. The latter includes the Western Development Project that can be considered both as a part of function (1) to build economic infra-structure and as function (4) to facilitate and redirect both public and private investment.

Personal Experience Working with the Chinese Government

Up to the late 1970s, my evaluation of the PRC government was largely negative. Like other outside observers, I knew the mistakes it had made as have been reported in Chapter 1, and I disagreed with many of its stated policies and principles. It was through many visits to China since 1980, observing and working with government officials that my opinion has turned more positive. Since the late 1970s, the Chinese government itself has changed. This section records some of my personal experiences. I have worked mainly with officials of the Ministry of Education (State Education Commission in the period 1985–1999) and the State Commission for Reconstructing the Economic System (now playing a less important role and being a part of the State Development and Reform Commission). In some 50 visits to China, I have met hundreds of government officials, educators and researchers, including central government officials, provincial governors, city mayors, managers of state enterprises and banks, heads and administrators of the Chinese Academy of Social Science and the Chinese Academy of Science, and presidents and administrators of universities.

My first serious encounter with officials from the Ministry of Education occurred when a group led by the Director of its Bureau for Economic and Legal Education and the Director of its Bureau of Foreign Affairs led a delegation to visit Princeton University in October 1983. The Chinese Ministry of Education was then one of the 50 some ministries of the State Council. The number of ministries, each corresponding to a department in the US government, was so large because under central planning each important industry required a ministry to direct. There were ministries in charge of agriculture and fisheries, forestry, coal industry, petroleum industry, chemical industry, metallurgical industry, light industry, textile industry, machine-building industry, electronic industry, nuclear energy industry, aircraft industry, ammunitions industry, space industry, geology and mineral resources, water resources and electric power, and so forth. For a complete list of ministries, see Chow (2002, pp. 40–41). Each ministry is divided into departments. Under each department there are bureaus. The Bureau for Economic and Legal Education was under the Second Department for Higher Education. The director of this Bureau had authority over economic and legal education for all the universities in China that were under the control of the Ministry of Education. Each traveling delegation was accompanied or even led by the Chief of Foreign Affairs, who had control over the expenses and represented the group in dealing with foreign hosts (or foreign guests if the Bureau was hosting).

I had met Chinese government officials before. My first trip to China took place in the summer of 1980, when a group of seven economists led by Professor Lawrence Klein of the University of Pennsylvania were invited by the Chinese Academy of Social Science to give lectures in econometrics to a group of about 100 scholars aged from the thirties to the sixties. After lecturing in Beijing, I traveled to five cities and met many Chinese scholars, some working at the local branches of the Academy of Social Sciences that hosted us. I met Vice Premier and Chairman of the State Planning Commission Yao Yilin. He impressed me as capable and having an understanding of the working of the market economy, but I have to qualify that one meeting for half an hour was not sufficient for me to make a reliable judgment. When I met Vice Premier Yao, I was eager to tell him that the central planning system was not efficient and that the state enterprises should be given autonomy to make their own production decisions. After my speech of about an entire minute, Vice Premier Yao nodded his head and smiled, saying "I agree with you." I realized that I failed to appreciate his understanding of economics through years of directing economic planning in China. In the summer of 1982, I spent over one month lecturing in five major universities in China, but met mostly university people and administrators and scholars in the Chinese Academy of Social Science. I found a number of capable administrators in both the universities and the Academy, giving me an impression that the system for selecting administrators was fairly good in general.

It was the delegation from the Ministry of Education visiting Princeton on October 20–21, 1983 that greatly impressed me. The two bureau directors came to my home after a dinner hosted by the University and told me that they planned to modernize economic education in China. I was excited by this idea. At the time only Marxian and socialist economics was taught in China. To introduce the ideas of modern economics and to teach the functioning of a market economy in China was so appealing to me that I offered to organize three summer workshops in 1984–1986 to teach microeconomics, macroeconomics and econometrics respectively. These are the three required subjects in the first-year graduate program towards a PhD degree in economics in all major American universities. The two guests in my home readily agreed to my offer and the Director of Foreign Affairs promised to finance these summer workshops, which they called symposiums. (Later I had to obtain financing through the support of Princeton University President William Bowen and Alfred P. Sloan Foundation President Albert Rees.) For three years between 1984 and 1986, especially in the summers, I worked with these education officials as a team to prepare and run the summer symposiums.

A more detailed description of my working relationships with Chinese government officials in charge of economics education and economic reform can be found in Chow (1994, Chapters 4 and 5). Through these symposiums and other cooperative programs in the 1990s, I have had close working relations with a large numbers of officials in the Ministry of Education including several ministers and vice ministers. In a second cooperative effort, I helped place Chinese graduate students to study towards a PhD degree in economics in the United States and Canada. These students needed to pass an examination administered by the Ministry of Education with exam questions in economics based on the text Chow (1985)

Discussing economics education and price reform with Premier Zhao Ziyang (1st from right), July 5, 1984

and provided by me, known unofficially as the "Chow test." As a third cooperative effort, two one-year graduate economics training centers in Beijing and in Shanghai were established with financial support from the Ford Foundation and administered jointly by a Chinese Committee and a US Committee which I co-chaired. Through these years of working relations, I found my colleagues in the Ministry of Education very able and open-minded.

My second close working relation was with the State Commission for Reconstructing the Economic System responsible for economic reform in China. The Commission was established in 1982, with Premier Zhao Ziyang serving as its chairman. In the middle 1980s it was the most important Commission in the State Council, listed above the State Planning Commission, which had previously been at the top, and the State Education Commission (elevated from the Ministry of Education in 1985). It was headed by the Premier while the State Planning Commission was headed only by a Vice Premier. Economic reform was considered the most important task of the Chinese government. I found the Premier to be extremely able, probably the most able political leader that I have met.

In May 2001 as I was conversing with Milton Friedman in Chicago, we remembered Premier Zhao fondly. Briefly reviewing his accomplishment, I said I had to give him an A. Friedman looked at me and responded, "What do you mean an A? It is an A+." I paused for a moment and corrected myself. "Yes, A+," I said. A+ is the correct assessment. My more conservative judgment is based on two events in which I thought Premier Zhao, and later General Secretary Zhao, could have done better. One was the serious inflation in 1988 generated under his premiership. The second was the handling of the demonstrators in Tiananmen in 1989. The occupation of Tiananmen was allowed to last so long without an appropriate solution while he was the General Secretary. In fact he became the victim of the very tragic event on June 4, 1989. Nevertheless he should take some responsibility for failing to handle the situation. However, I realize that his acute economic sense, his quick response in discussions and his role as a very capable leader in transforming China's planned economy to a market economy, as testified by many government officials that I met, were unsurpassed. Let me leave the A+ evaluation for the purpose of the present discussion.

I first met Premier Zhao in June 1984 during the symposium on microeconomics held at Beijing University. We spoke for about 45 minutes on economic education and economic reform, especially reform of the price system. I also brought up the question of the future of Hong Kong. I wrote to him after our meeting on China's foreign exchange system, a subject too sensitive for me to bring up when there were other people present at our meeting. In July 1985, the Premier invited my family members (my wife Paula, our son James and our daughter Mei Mei) and me for dinner. We discussed many subjects but the most important was his remark suggesting that I invite overseas economists to work on economic reform. I thought, quite naively, that the dinner was purely a social event and

I was very relaxed, drinking a lot of *Maotai*. When I heard that remark, I did not know how to respond and tried to buy time by saying "how can we work on economic reform when there are not enough economic data?" I told him that I had visited the State Statistical Bureau and could not find certain economic data. He said, "They did not necessarily tell you all the data they had." The conversation on this topic ended there. Only after my return to Princeton did I realize the importance of the Premier's remark. I immediately sent him a letter (handwritten in Chinese and mailed through the US Postal Service, as I did many times later) to remind him of that remark and offered to help. He responded in writing and suggested that I get in touch with the Vice Chair of the State Commission for Reconstructing the Economic System and a second leading member of the Commission. A copy of his letter can be found in Chow (1994, p. 98). Subsequently I worked intensively with these two officials and their close colleagues in the Commission in January 1986, July 1986 and March 1989.

The first meeting on economic reform with Commission officials and overseas economists took place in Hong Kong in January 1986, lasting five full days with discussions sometimes continuing at dinner. The second meeting took place in Beijing in July 1986 and also lasted five full days. The March 1989 meeting was again in Hong Kong, lasting about three days, with the control of inflation being the main issue. The selection of Hong Kong as a location was due to my desire to invite friends who had served as economic advisors to the leaders and top government officials in Taiwan, beginning with President Chiang Kai-shek. They were among the best economists who could speak Chinese and understood economic policy issues in a Chinese cultural setting. We had spent many summers together from the late 1960s to the late 1970s in Taipei to provide economic advice to the government of the Republic of China. Some were still very active in advising the government in Taiwan and could not conveniently go to Mainland China at the time. During the meetings with the economic officials of the PRC, we spent long hours together discussing various issues of economic reform. The subjects covered were comprehensive, including the reform of the price system, the state enterprises, the banking and financial system, foreign investment and foreign trade (exchange rate policy included), special economic zones, urban housing and so forth. It is from these intense meetings, and several more meetings with the Premier himself, and from written communications with them that I learned how able some of the top government officials in China were.

After the tragic event of Tiananmen on June 4, 1989 Zhao Ziyang was no longer General Secretary, but my work with the State Education Commission had to go on. A meeting of the members of US and Chinese Committees working on economic education and research in China had been scheduled in Beijing in August 1989. All five members of the US Committee who had committed to go to Beijing were present, in spite of the statement of the President of the National Academy of Science urging the suspension of cultural exchange with China. We thought we had important business to attend to in China. Our trip turned out to be essential in enabling our work to promote modern economics education in China to continue. The work involved the operation of the graduate economics training centers at the Chinese Renmin University in Beijing and at Fudan University in Shanghai, the former to continue until 1996 when financial support from the Ford Foundation terminated, and other exchange activities mentioned earlier. Our colleagues on the Chinese Committee frankly told us that there was uncertainty at the time concerning the directions of government policies, including policies on exchange activities with the United States. Our visit ensured them and higher government officials that we were serious in our intention to continue our cooperation. In fact the two sides decided to sign an agreement to cooperate for three more years, beginning from August 1989, even though the existing three-year contract had not expired.

Soon after our arrival in Beijing in August 1989, I received a phone call in the evening, inviting me to meet with General Secretary Jiang Zemin. The invitation was extended to the other four visiting members of the US Committee as well. I mentioned the invitation to my colleagues at breakfast the next morning. All four decided not to go. Thus I went alone to see the General Secretary, a photo of that meeting being posted in my website www.princeton.edu/~gchow (printed on p. 92). Later I met with General Secretary and President Jiang again, with Premier Zhu Rongji, several Vice Premiers and many middle level officials in the Chinese government. President Jiang and Premier Zhu are well known to many Americans who can form their own opinion about the performance of these top leaders.

From my own experience, the quality of Chinese government officials are in general quite good. Several factors have contributed to the high quality of these officials. When economic reform started, the leadership of the Communist Party decided to place the educated people with a university degree in responsible positions. Almost all officials at or above the level of bureau directors have a university degree. Secondly, during the period when he was Premier and General Secretary, Zhao Ziyang selected capable people to serve in the government and these people were not replaced, except for a few, after the Tiananmen incident. Third, China has a very large population from which able people can be selected, and the selection process in the government is good. It was the high competence of the Chinese government officials that guided the successful reform of China's economic and educational institutions. They have provided law and order to China. They have played an important role in instilling pride to the Chinese people. Under their leadership China's economy has grown rapidly and China has gained an important position in the community of nations. For the Chinese people these achievements are commendable although some Chinese feel that the performance of some top government officials could have been better.

On Corruption

Ability and performance aside, many Chinese government officials are corrupt. To the extent that the people are very dissatisfied with corruption, it can destroy the social fabric and lead to political instability. The government considers corruption a serious problem and has tried very hard to stop it, but has had only limited success. The reason for corruption is that there are many opportunities for government bureaucrats and managers of state-owned enterprises and commercial banks to confer economic benefits to the population, and thus to extract payments for the benefits they confer. Corruption occurs when payments are extracted against the rules or against accepted practice. This definition depends on the rules or accepted practice under the circumstances corruption takes place.

In general the compensation of Chinese government officials is low as compared with the income of people of similar ability working in the private sector. Chinese citizens will not complain if some government officials extract moderate payments from people in the private sector for rendering satisfactory services according to the rules or accepted practice, payments that the people would almost volunteer to give for the services. They would object and consider it corruption if unreasonable payments were extracted or if government officials diverted large sums of public funds to their personal accounts. Although corruption is a serious problem in China, the vast majority of government officials are not corrupt partly because they do not have opportunities in their jobs to confer economic benefits and partly because receiving a moderate and reasonable compensation is not considered corruption. (A bureau chief in the Ministry of Education who can decide on the economics curriculum for all major universities is in no position to extract payments from individual professors or economics department chairpersons since no one will pay him to alter the planned curriculum.)

Many business people are prepared and accustomed to offer bribes to get the job done. Bribing is treated as a cost of doing business in many parts of Asia. On the other hand there are also serious cases when very large sums of money were diverted to the private accounts of some top government bureaucrats or managers of state-owned enterprises or banks. This can seriously affect the proper functioning of the government department or the enterprise concerned. There is a gray line between proper behavior and corruption. In the US some CEOs (Chief Executive Officers) receive large sums of money (including the market value of stock options and other benefits) for their services. A CEO of a Chinese state enterprise of comparable size, who receives a much smaller total compensation inclusive of bribes, may or may not be charged with corruption depending on circumstances.

We can discuss bribery by treating it as a form of payment and ask whether and in what way this form of payment is improper. As a form of payment, a worker may receive a fixed amount per week, or an amount according to the quantity of output or service he produces, or a combination of the two. A waiter in a restaurant receives a fixed payment per day from the restaurant manager and possibly a larger payment in the form of tips from the customers. This system of payment is accepted. Perhaps we can interpret the compensation to certain Chinese government officials as consisting of two parts, a regular salary and payment for extra services performed. If a government official is willing to provide more services beyond the call of duty to individuals who are willing to pay for the services, the payment system is beneficial to both parties. Chinese doctors are considered public servants working in public hospitals. They receive a fixed wage per month from the hospital, unlike most American doctors in private practice who charge by the service performed. Recently it has been suggested that Chinese doctors should receive additional payments according to the number of patients treated. One may compare a Chinese civil servant to a Chinese doctor. Both can vary the amount of service performed. If the doctor should get extra pay for extra work, perhaps the civil servant also should.

In this interpretation, I assume that the government official receiving payment from a citizen actually performs a service. A service is performed because the citizen is willing to pay for it. Suppose that the government official has to make a decision on the allocation of some public resource. The resource may be a piece of public land, a loan from a bank owned by the government, or an import or export license, for example. If the resource belongs to the government, but the official collects payment for himself while allocating the resource, it can be considered corruption in the sense of selling government property for personal gains. Even in such a situation receiving certain payment might not necessarily be considered corruption if it is a compensation within an established payment system, perhaps implicitly, by the government to pay its officials.

Historically, when an emperor in the Qing dynasty assigned a township to an official to administer, the collection of some fees is a part of his privileges. (In fact depending on the income generated there was a well-established price to pay for acquiring such a position, besides the usual qualifications in passing imperial examinations.) The Chinese government does not have sufficient revenues to pay salaries to government officials comparable to the salaries in the private sector. It might consider moderate payments to government officials by citizens receiving extra services as reasonable practice. If a government official is willing to pay special attention to certain citizens in solving their problems, he may expect some compensation in return. The compensation may not be monetary, which can be considered bribery, but in the form of service or favors by the citizens. The amount of reasonable compensation varies from case to case. The above may have described some aspects of corruption under the current Chinese government compensation system.

In recent years the Chinese government has tried to deal with the corruption problem mainly by discipline and punishment. The Communist Party has waged campaigns repeatedly to instruct

Party members serving in the government to come clean. The government has exposed serious cases of corruption in newspapers and imposed severe punishment to the offenders including the death penalty. The problem has not been solved because economic gains for the offenders can be very large, and many are willing to take the risk and hope that they will not be caught. Unless economic incentives for corruption are reduced, such as by increasing the regular salaries to government officials, the problem is not likely to go away. Since the mid-1980s the Chinese government has recognized the problem of low salaries and the need for economic incentives when it encouraged government officials to engage in market activities to increase their incomes, such as establishing a business enterprise as a part of a government ministry. One important way to reduce the opportunity for corruption is to reduce the role of the government appropriately, such as by allowing the private sector to operate more freely without government regulation or licensing.

The harm of corruption to society is mainly psychological and political and not economic. The diversion of public funds, though large in terms of individual incomes, is small from the viewpoint of total economic resources available for economic development, and China's rapid economic growth is dependent on the three fundamental economic factors that we have discussed in Chapter 3. The positive effects of these three factors dwarf the negative economic effects of corruption. However, corruption has created much resentment and caused much dissatisfaction with the government. How likely it will lead to political instability is difficult to say. Even though corruption is a serious problem, most Chinese would prefer the present economic system with more corrupted officials than the planning system before 1978, when there were fewer opportunities for government officials to be corrupted, but also fewer opportunities for the Chinese people to make money. In the meantime the government is doing a satisfactory job in preserving law and order for the Chinese people to better themselves so that most would like it to stay on to manage the current system.

On Political Reform

What are the prospects of political reform towards a more democratic government in China? In the period of 1997–2001, Chinese leaders including Jiang Zemin previous President/General Secretary of the Chinese Communist Party and Zhu Rongji (previous Prime Minister) repeatedly told Party members and the Chinese people that one of the most important goals of the Party and the Chinese government was to establish a democratic political system. In these statements they openly acknowledged that China's political system was not sufficiently democratic. It would be interesting to follow the future course of this development and see how well and how fast the Chinese political system will improve.

In observing the progress towards a more democratic government in China, one should expect it to be a slow process. We can recall that the historical development of a more democratic government in the United States has also been a slow process. The improvement of the American democratic system has taken over 200 years, from the time of slavery, racial inequality and segregation and denying women the right to vote to the present state. This has all happened without changing the name of the democratic government and the open declaration that "all men are created equal." The progress in developing a Chinese democracy cannot be very much faster.

Nevertheless, we can expect China's government to become more democratic in allowing the citizens more freedom and more opportunities to select government officials and to serve in the government. The progress will come from both the demand for and the supply of democratic institutions. On the demand side, as the Chinese people have more economic power and become more educated, they will demand to have more freedom and influence in governmental affairs. On the supply side, the Chinese Communist Party and government officials will become better informed of the modern political systems of the world. As they acquire confidence and ability to govern a modern society in the course of further economic progress, they will be more willing and able to adopt democratic institutions. The change towards a more democratic government has been observed in the proliferation of popular elections in villages, the increasingly independent behavior of members of the National People's Congress from directions of the Communist Party and the improvement in the practice of the rule of law. The improved practice of the rule of law is partly a result of China's need to deal with foreign corporations in international trade and investment.

The October 2, 2003 issue of *New York Times* (p. A12) carried an article entitled "China's Leader Calls for 'Democratic' Changes" and reported that President and General Secretary Hu Jintao, in an address to the governing Politburo, said the Communist Party must undertake a "sweeping systemic project" to increase public participation in government and enforce the rule of law.

> "We must enrich the forms of democracy, make democratic procedures complete, expand citizen's orderly political participation, and ensure that the people can exercise democratic elections, democratic administration and democratic scrutiny."

This appears to be a sign of progress towards a more democratic government. Americans accustomed to a democratic government under a two-party system might find it difficult to appreciate a democratic government under a one-party system, but I believe that election of government officials and of members of the People's Congress is possible if the Communist Party is willing to put up the best candidates who may be non-Party members for election to the positions in question. Under a one-party system there are ways that citizens can participate in and influence political affairs. China might well turn out to be an innovator of one form of democratic government under a one-party system.

A recent example that the Chinese government can improve from experience is its handling of the problem of SARS (severe acute respiratory syndrome). On June 8, 2003, when the SARS problem had mostly subsided, the *People's Daily* carried an article entitled "SARS, a valuable lesson for the Chinese government to learn." This article states in part as follows:

"The Chinese government has not, in the past, been accustomed to public disclosure of its activities. Unfortunately a long-held but outdated conviction among many top public servants dictated that information could also cause possible social panic and disorder. Hence, information was controlled, which was just what happened at the onset of the SARS outbreak... Only when central government ordered local governments and public health authorities to come clean on their epidemic reporting and sacked some officials did the situation improve and the public anxiety was calmed. These facts clearly demonstrate that only by actively upholding the citizens' right to know can the government be better supervised by the public and in turn win the trust and respect of those it serves.

"People are made aware of government's views through the information it releases, and they exercise their rightful supervision not only through related government agencies but also through the media, which helps keep the government abreast of public opinion. Therefore, an interactive relationship among government, citizens and the media should be put in place so that the government knows the viewpoints of the people about its policies... The right afforded to the media and law to supervise should be fully guaranteed. When such a right is firmly in place, the activities of those in power come under public scrutiny, thus government and officials become publicly accountable for what they do and therefore more likely to work to higher standards."

Publicly acknowledging the need for government accountability and openness and for the supervisory role of a free press is an important step towards putting these ideas into practice in a democratic government.

6

Hong Kong and Shanghai: Two Modern Cities

China has many interesting cities. Beijing and Xi'an come to mind. I have singled out Hong Kong and Shanghai for discussion in this chapter in order to emphasize their current dynamic growth, while cities like Beijing and Xi'an are distinguished mainly by their past history. Beijing and Xi'an will be discussed in Chapter 8 as possible sites for tourists to visit. In this chapter I take a somewhat comparative or even competitive view to describe these two cities, as some of their residents do. People have ranked cities in the United States by a host of factors. Among them are climate, environmental conditions, transportation facilities, job and career opportunities, the quality of cultural activities, the availability of good restaurants, the school system, etc. According to a certain ranking, Pittsburgh was the most desirable city over all. Here I discuss the distinguishing characteristics of these two cities in comparison with each other and with some other cities.

Hong Kong

Tourists visiting Hong Kong for the first time are often impressed by this city in many ways. They may even rank Hong Kong as the best city in certain respects.

Ranked First in Economic Freedom

First, it has been suggested that Hong Kong has the best free market system. Milton Friedman once said this when he visited Hong Kong. Hong Kong is ranked number one in terms of economic freedom by two sources. One is *Economic Freedom of the World* published by the Frazer Institute and the Cato Institute. The other is *The Economic Index of Economic Freedom in the World*, published by the Heritage Foundation and the *Wall Street Journal*. Hong Kong has received the number one ranking for a number of years before and after 1997 up to 2002, the year this paragraph was written. (The number one ranking remains in 2003 as I can add while proofreading this paragraph.) Why this top ranking? The Hong Kong government has allowed the free market to function with minimum interference. Possible interferences, some being practiced in the United States, include government subsidies to farmers, a social security system that forces the population to put their savings under the control of the government (invested in government securities and not in other assets at the discretion of the people), interference of business behavior in the name of anti-trust legislation (with the Justice Department suing a company such as IBM for violating anti-trust laws), progressive income tax which may discourage hard work and entrepreneurship, high tariffs on imports to protect domestic industries, and so forth. The Hong Kong government did none of that although the recent introduction of a social security system might be considered an exception. Hong Kong has a flat rate of about 17 percent to tax wage income above a certain amount. Hong Kong residents earning about US$14,000 per year or below are exempted from this taxation.

A Spectacular Harbor View

Second, Hong Kong has a spectacular harbor. Looking at the Hong Kong harbor, one finds water and mountains lined with a variety of skyscrapers to provide spectacular views from different angles. Hong Kong consists of Hong Kong Island in the south and Kowloon Peninsula in the north with a harbor in between. The view facing north from Victoria Peak, the top of Hong Kong Island's highest mountain, overlooks the residential buildings down the slope and the commercial buildings on the northern shore of the island, the harbor decorated with boats and ships, and the buildings on the Kowloon Peninsula surrounded by mountains behind. This is a favorite view of the tourists. The next favorite is facing south from the peninsula overlooking the harbor and the remarkable layers of skyscrapers on the island. Some prefer a closer view of the harbor in order to see its activities more clearly from a hotel or from the park along the edge of the water. The third most favored spot to view the harbor and its surrounding is a seat on the Star Ferry crossing the harbor. One can look at any direction and distance as one wishes. The harbor view can be appreciated during the day but in the evening it is decorated with a large variety of harbor lights and advertising signs shining in many directions.

Sightseeing in Hong Kong is not confined to the harbor views. One finds natural beauty and points of interest in the New Territory north of Kowloon Peninsula and bordering the Special Economic Zone Shenzhen, which is a part of the Chinese Mainland. The New Territory is so-called because it was leased to the British government in 1898 for 99 years, while Hong Kong Island was ceded to the British by the Treaty of Nanking signed after China was defeated in the Opium War of 1840–42. Many tourists may not be aware of a large public park in the Saigon area located in the northeast part of the New Territory, which is surrounded by mountains and pristine beaches. One could walk for an hour in the park along mountain trails without seeing another person. There are beautiful beaches with clean waters and practically no swimmers most of the time. In the New Territory there are also old villages preserving the old culture and traditions of the past.

Outstanding Economic Infrastructure

Third, besides the beautiful harbor view and other points of interest, Hong Kong has an excellent economic infrastructure. There is a world-class International Airport, completed in 1997. The architecture is outstanding. The scale is grand. Air traffic is connected to all major cities in the world and to Mainland China with convenient flight schedules. From the airport there is a fast train to other parts of Hong Kong. It takes only twenty minutes to reach the "central" area of Hong Kong Island, the business center and one of the many shopping areas. Shipping by tankers and containers to Hong Kong is very convenient and has an extremely high volume of traffic, ranked among the top in the world. The local transportation system is excellent. The subway transit system is extremely fast and clean, with trains running almost continuously to and from all major locations of the City of Hong Kong, including parts of the New Territory. It is supplemented by connecting buses to almost all parts of the city. Taxis are available and inexpensive. A resident does not need to own a car to satisfy his local transportation needs. The trains to the City of Guangzhou about 130 miles north are fast, clean and convenient. From Guangzhou one can go by train to other Chinese cities.

The cultural aspects of Hong Kong's economic infrastructure include eight universities, some with first-rate departments in certain academic disciplines as judged by the quality of the faculty. All these universities are supported by the government. The government has placed strong emphasis on higher education in Hong Kong and is willing to pay competitive salary to the faculty to attract qualified people in the world market to teach in Hong Kong. Hong Kong has a large and modern convention center, used for the Handover ceremony when sovereignty was returned to China on July 1, 1997, and other activities. The City Hall facing the harbor on the northern shore of the Hong Kong Island, is used for arts exhibition and cultural performances. An exhibition hall in the southern tip of Kowloon is frequented by many residents and tourists.

Hong Kong's legal and financial systems are recognized to be excellent. The legal system follows the British common law tradition. It has been essentially preserved after the change of sovereignty in 1997. The Basic Law of Hong Kong was adopted by the People's Congress in Beijing in 1990 to preserve Hong Kong's economic and legal system under the "one country two systems" policy. Article 8 of Chapter I stipulates that "The laws previously in force in Hong Kong, that is, the common law, rules of equity, ordinances, subordinate legislation and customary law shall be maintained, except for any that contravene this Law, and subject to any amendment by the legislature of the Hong Kong Special Administrative Region." Opinions of Hong Kong residents and foreign observers differ regarding how successfully this principle has been put into practice since 1997, but most would tend to agree that the legal system in Hong Kong is very good. The excellent financial system is partly demonstrated by the presence of a large number of multinational corporations which have chosen Hong Kong to locate their regional headquarters.

Food and Quality of Life

Fourth, concerning the remaining aspects of the quality of life, food in Hong Kong is excellent. Hong Kong markets provide very good and fresh seafood, meat and vegetables for home cooking. The restaurants serve Chinese food of different provinces as well as food of many other countries. The quality is excellent according to many tourists. It is a metropolitan city where English can be used and where different nationalities are well represented. However, the international residents are not well integrated with the Chinese residents. Both groups tend to socialize among themselves, although international social interactions do exist. One drawback in the quality of life is that the air is not very clean because of the large amount of emission from automobiles and the polluted air from factories north of Hong Kong. It is very densely populated. Some visitors may not be comfortable with the congestion in a busy street. On the other hand, some Hong Kong residents traveling abroad say that they miss the congestion and the noise of Hong Kong.

Dynamism of Hong Kong

Fifth, Hong Kong is one of the most dynamic cities in the world. Hong Kong people go at a tremendous speed in their business endeavors. New York is considered a very fast moving city, but some may consider Hong Kong to be even faster. Hong Kong is dynamic also in the sense that new things are happening continuously. New buildings have sprouted up in the last three decades at a much more rapid rate than in New York. People want to have the latest in consumer products — cars, audio and video equipment, house furnishing, watches and fashionable clothing. No time is wasted for fear of missing business opportunities. The TV stations broadcast financial news continuously, much more so than in New York. The high speed in doing business is one aspect of the commercial culture that we discussed in Chapter 4.

The British government deserves credit in making Hong Kong the way it is today. It has built the number one free market system in Hong Kong and provided law and order as well as the physical infrastructure. The Chinese living in Hong Kong also deserve much credit for building Hong Kong into what it is. They are the hard working labor force with good working ethics and the entrepreneurs who have flourished under the free market system. Another factor is the string of actions taken by the Chinese government since 1949, first driving out many talented people from the Mainland to Hong Kong, second closing the door to foreign trade and commerce and leaving Hong Kong the only city along the China coast for foreign trade and investment, and finally the economic reform since 1978 to facilitate rapid economic development in China. Since 1978, a richer China has benefited Hong Kong as a gateway to and from China. China has also provided Hong Kong with excellent investment opportunities.

In Chapter 4 when I discussed the people of Hong Kong, I mentioned that under the British rule they were not interested in politics because they had limited opportunities to participate in it. Now that they are given the opportunity to govern themselves, there is the downside that as a group they may not yet be prepared to maintain a stable political and social environment for the economy to remain as dynamic as before.

Shanghai

Dynamic Growth

The rapid economic growth of Shanghai since the early 1990s is a most spectacular phenomenon in city development in history. Such rapid development is made possible by the technology now available. When New York or Paris was built, it was much harder to add a new building, a new road, or a new telephone line than what Shanghai could do in the last decade. Not only could the physical infrastructure be built at a faster rate by the use of modern technology, the use of new technology in many other areas, including telecommunication in particular, helps increase the speed and quality of the overall economic development. Shanghai people en mass started using cell phones without the need to build a wired system. By the use of a modern communication system, they can speed up other aspects of the economic development of Shanghai.

Any one who has traveled to Shanghai in recent years can testify to its phenomenal growth. The city looks different every two to three months. In the early 1990s many people in Hong Kong and the rest of the world could not imagine that Shanghai would catch up with Hong Kong in one to two decades, being mindful of the fact that Hong Kong itself was rapidly growing. This has indeed happened in many respects. Even if some Hong Kong people disagree with this assessment, they may tend to agree that it will soon happen, depending partly on the criteria used to rank the two cities. Besides the availability of modern technology there are two important factors contributing to Shanghai's rapid development. These are the unusual talents of the Shanghai people as a group and the support of government policy. Perhaps the former is more important as I will elaborate below.

Advantage From a Rich Cultural Tradition

The people of Shanghai as a group are very talented in business endeavors as compared with those from other regions of China for historical reasons. If innate abilities from genetics are about the same among people of different regions, their other differences are the result of environment and historical tradition. The Shanghai people are fortunate to have a cultural tradition favorable for economic development. This tradition dates back to the flourishing market economy during the Song dynasty of 960–1126 when the capital city in the later Song period was in Hangzhou, a city near Shanghai. During that period Guangdong, Hong Kong being a part of it, was much less developed. A very famous scholar and government official Su Shi lost favor with the imperial government and was given an assignment in Hainan island, a part of Guangdong, as a punishment. People in other parts of China did not have the same opportunities to learn and practice capitalism as the people near Shanghai did. Besides having the capitalist tradition dated back to the Song period, Shanghai benefited in the first decades of the 20th century from the influence of foreign governments which occupied parts of the city and of foreign citizens who lived and worked there. The foreign governments set good examples in urban planning and building social and economic institutions. They taught the Shanghai people to build good roads and modern buildings, and to set up modern banks and factories. They have also become more open to foreign ideas which is a favorable trait for economic development.

In the 1930s Shanghai became the most advanced modern metropolitan city in Asia, ahead of Tokyo and Hong Kong. Per capita income in Shanghai was higher than in Hong Kong.

The universities were better. Hong Kong then had only one university, the Hong Kong University. People were more well-dressed as admitted by the Hong Kong people who tried to follow Shanghainese fashions. Shanghainese industries and financial institutions were also better developed. One can measure the relative development by considering the total output of manufacturing industries, the total value of deposits in commercial banks, the total market value of factories and commercial banks, the total profits of factories and banks, etc., in each of the two cities. By any of these criteria, Shanghai's industrial and financial establishments were more developed than Hong Kong's when the latter already had an excellent free market system.

After 1949 Shanghai immigrants to Hong Kong built new factories and set up commercial and financial business enterprises. At that time Hong Kong did not have much manufacturing activity. The Shanghai talents helped build Hong Kong's economy from the 1950s to the 1970s. Today, the Shanghai people are utilizing their talents to build their own city in a way almost unimaginable for most outside observers in the late 1980s. While the Hong Kong workers have very good skills, the Shanghai workers are generally considered to be better. Partly because of the high quality of the labor force, Ford Motors and General Motors chose to build their plants in Shanghai. The quality of the white-collar workers was also a consideration for their decisions. The graduates of universities in Shanghai can serve as technical personnel, scientists and engineers, to support a manufacturing establishment. Foreign investors have chosen Shanghai for their investment projects in spite of its less modern legal and financial institutions as compared with Hong Kong's. Shanghai does have a geographical advantage if one wants to reach the markets of central China.

Another factor contributing to the rapid growth of Shanghai is the new policy of the central government. The government in recent years provided financial support for the development of Shanghai, while it had taxed Shanghai heavily up to the late 1980s to support the development of the rest of the country. Government subsidy in recent years is an important factor for Shanghai's development but the ability of the Shanghai people to utilize the available financial resources is more important. The central government has poured much more money in other regions, including the western region, without comparable results. It has provided the province of Guangdong with a very favorable economic policy for a long time and yet within a decade or so, Shanghai as a city already surpassed Guangzhou in terms of per capita income and some other attributes to be discussed below.

The Market System

Consider the market system of Shanghai. In terms of fulfilling the criteria of a modern western market economy, Hong Kong fares better. The rule of law, the transparency of the accounting system, the behavior and institutional characteristics of commercial banks, the free flow of international capital, etc., are better in Hong Kong. The difference in the quality of economic institutions is smaller than it might first appear if one allows for the cultural differences in the way business is conducted in the two cities. The business culture in Shanghai has a more Chinese leaning than in Hong Kong. Rules governing business in Shanghai and Hong Kong are different. The Shanghai people seem to know and are accustomed to their own rules. They can conduct their business perhaps as efficiently as the people in Hong Kong who rely on the more developed Western rules and institutions. The Shanghai economic institutions may be defective according to Western standards but may be adequate to suit the needs of the Shanghai people in conducting their economic activities.

This point echoes my discussion in Chapter 3 on how a set of legal and economic institutions that differ from the Western institutions can serve the Chinese market economy well. To indicate the effectiveness of these institutions, one may point out that so many Shanghai people have become successful and rich in the last ten years and generated a corresponding amount of national income. From their economic success, one is tempted to conclude that they have their ways to do business in the environment of their economic institutions. An interesting statistical analysis to show the efficacy of Shanghai's economic institutions would be to compare the total wealth accumulated by the top 100 Shanghai entrepreneurs in the last eight years with the corresponding figure for Hong Kong. Corresponding statistics can also shed some light on the relative growth of Shanghai and Hong Kong as compared with other major cities in the world.

Infrastructure

Before discussing its infrastructure I should briefly touch upon the physical beauty of Shanghai since I have singled out the beautiful views of the Hong Kong harbor. The view of the Shanghai bund, along the Yangtze River, is also very beautiful, especially with the new construction and face lifting in recent years. The views along the river may not quite match the views of the Hong Kong harbor. The natural beauty of a harbor surrounded by mountains decorated with skyscrapers seems more appealing than a river view without surrounding mountains. The river view is still very attractive, and may be as attractive as the views of New York City from across the Hudson or East River.

The quality of city planning in Shanghai since 1990 has been remarkable. The Shanghai streets were transformed in one decade. There are now beautiful stores, excellent restaurants and modern office buildings along the sides of Shanghai streets. The area around the bund is beautified. There is a park for people to enjoy. The most striking is the development of Pudong that used to be a village on the opposite shore of the metropolitan city. It has now become a modern commercial, financial and industrial city, surpassing the old parts of Shanghai in many ways because it is newly built. One skyscraper was built after another, changing the scene dramatically every three months or half a year. Modern factories, banks and other business establishments sprouted up alongside the skyscrapers. Shanghai's urban transport system was modernized. Above ground highways were constructed. A new subway system was built and is in the process of being extended. Shanghai people can travel to different parts of the city very conveniently and rapidly using public transportation.

In 2002, a modern high-speed train system was built, providing convenient transportation to the airport. It now takes only 13 minutes to get to the airport from downtown Shanghai, whereas it used to take more than one hour by taxi. The technology had been invented in Germany more than half a century ago, but had not been put into practical use. People in Shanghai cooperated with the Germans to build the railway using this technology within two years. The speed of construction was remarkable considering the sophistication of the technology with its demanding technical and engineering requirements. The Shanghai government obtained several key patents in the process of constructing this train system.

With the help of modern technology, the modern infrastructure can be built rapidly and with high quality. The case of the telephone system using cell phones is an example. It was built up very rapidly, and did not require costly wiring. In a period of less than five years, the majority of the residents of Shanghai had acquired their cell phones. In the entire China in 2002 there were 360 million cell phones, or about 28 phones for one hundred persons in a total population of 1.3 billion.

The universities in Shanghai are outstanding. Among them Fudan and Jiaotong are well recognized. Science in Fudan and engineering in Jiaotong are world-class. Their graduates are sought after by the top graduate programs in the United States. When I cooperated with the Chinese Ministry of Education to recruit graduate students to study economics in the United States, in the class which entered in September 1985 were four Fudan students occupying the top ten positions on my list of candidates to be placed. Some are now well-known economists in the United States. In the 1980s I also sensed a cultural difference between the faculty and students in Fudan and in Peking University. In Peking University where I gave a seminar, only the senior faculty members raised questions and made comments. In Fudan, junior faculty members and graduate students did not hesitate in raising questions and making comments. This might be an indication of the vitality of the Shanghai people inherited from their cultural heritage.

Cultural Activities

The Shanghai Museum of Art stands out among similar museums in the world. In terms of architectural design and the exhibits, it is excellent. Its collection has come from all over China. The collection might not be as rich as the one in the Palace Museum in Taipei, for the Taipei Museum has benefited from collections under the mandate of Chinese emperors over many generations. However, the Shanghai Museum could acquire its exhibits from the entire Chinese Mainland which spans a vast area. The new Shanghai Opera House was designed by a first-rate French architect. Together with the new high-speed train system, it shows that the Shanghai people desire and acquire the best in the world. The city government is willing to spend exorbitant sums on the Museum, the Opera House, the train and subway systems, and any new project that would help make Shanghai one of the best modern cities in the world.

The Shanghai people set their sights high. They are willing to pay for cultural events. In January 2001, my wife and daughter visited Shanghai and stayed in the 88-story Grand Hyatt Hotel. They went to a performance in the Opera House, and found the tickets costing from 100 to 500 US dollars each. They bought the 100 dollar tickets, while the local Shanghai people took all the expensive tickets to fill the entire opera house, with very few foreign tourists in sight. The Shanghai people want the best, and they enjoy the best.

Economic Activities

In recent years, foreign investors have flooded into Shanghai to do all kinds of business. It is estimated that some 300,000 persons from Taiwan live in Shanghai in the beginning of 2003. Many set up a second home there. Some have even migrated to Shanghai to live even though they may still be holding a passport from Taiwan. The Taiwan investors have put their money in trade, in manufacturing and in financial activities in the last 15 years since they were permitted by their government to do so. American companies like Ford, General Motors, IBM, Intel and many others have built factories or set up branch offices there. Universal Studio chose Shanghai as the site of their next theme park. Alongside the foreign investors, the Shanghai people have engaged in domestic and foreign trade and in manufacturing and financial activities. The success of the Shanghai business people is witnessed by the list of 100 Chinese millionaires prepared by the *Fortune Magazine* in 1993 which contains many persons from Shanghai. Recognizing the business opportunities there, investors from Hong Kong have been active in Shanghai for years. At the beginning of the 21st century, many young people in Hong Kong have started looking for jobs in Shanghai, and many Hong Kong residents consider moving to Shanghai to live. The prosperity of the city is partly indicated by the rapid rise in the prices of both commercial and residential real estate in recent years in spite of the rapid increase in supply. Many people in the United States originally from Shanghai are considering moving back to Shanghai, and some have done so.

The annual growth rate of Shanghai's GDP from 1992 to 2001 was over 10 percent. In 2002 while the national GDP grew about 8 percent Shanghai's grew about 10 percent even when it was already the richest region of China. All economic activities in China will be pushed forward by competitive market forces as China has become a member of WTO. Competition from foreign investment will make domestic enterprises more efficient and innovative. In the meantime the Shanghai people will learn more from the foreign investors in all aspects of business. Foreign investors will appreciate and learn from the Shanghai business people as well.

Economic life in Shanghai is dynamic, as in Hong Kong. Dynamism is shown by the high speed at which things get done, buildings get built and infrastructures get completed. It is shown in the attitude and the spirit of the people who believe that things can get done quickly and done well, and by the confidence of the people that only the sky is the limit.

The Shanghai people are excited with the prospect of hosting the forthcoming World Exposition in 2010. This will give them another push to develop Shanghai even faster. People all over the world who intend to see the Fair will benefit from Shanghai as the host. Shanghai will put on a great show and demonstrate to the world that it is truly a great city.

A Country for Tourists

For an understanding of China, I will record some personal experiences from my visits and present my views on a few interesting places. This may also whet the appetite of readers and inspire them to visit China. Readers who have gone to China may enjoy seeing a different perspective of the places they have visited. This chapter is not a tourist guide. Plenty of guidebooks on China are available. A good guide book provides information on good hotels at different price ranges, a list of good restaurants for each kind of food, the means of transportation from one place to another, shops and stores for different consumer goods and so forth that is not available here.

China's Geography — a Map of China

In order to identify the locations of the different places mentioned in this chapter a map of China is shown. China is the third largest country in the world, after Russia and Canada, having 9.6 million square kilometers in land area. It is situated in the eastern and southeastern part of Asia, with its coast bordering the Pacific Ocean. It occupies one quarter of the area of Asia and one-fifteenth of the area of the globe. There are many climatic zones, varying from tropical and equatorial in the south to frigid-temperate in the north. There are mountains and plateaus in the west and plains and hilly areas in the coastal areas along the Pacific Ocean. Two great

rivers, the Yellow River and the Yangtze, flow from the west to the east. High rainfall is concentrated in the coastal areas. The country's farm land covers about one tenth of total land area. It is found mainly in the northeastern provinces, the north, areas around the Yangtze, and the Pearl River Delta in Guangdong Province. There are rich mineral deposits.

Administratively China is divided into 27 provinces or autonomous regions and four municipalities directly under the supervision of the central government. The former include 1) Hebei, 2) Shanxi, 3) Inner Mongolia [in the central north], 4) Liaoning, 5) Jilin, 6) Heilongjiang [in the northeast], 7) Jiangsu, 8) Zhejiang, 9) Anhui, 10) Fujian, 11) Jiangxi, 12) Shandong [along or close to the east coast], 13) Henan, 14) Hubei, 15) Hunan, 16) Guangdong, 17) Guangxi, 18) Hainan [in the middle and south], 19) Sichuan, 20) Guizhou, 21) Yunnan,

22) Tibet [in the west and southwest], 23) Shaanxi, 24) Gansu, 25) Qinghai, 26) Ningxia and 27) Xinjiang [in the northwest]. The last nine listed provinces in the western region are relatively poor and targeted for more rapid economic development in a national effort to equalize the incomes of different regions. Western development is a subject discussed in Chapter 3 in connection with income inequality. The municipalities include Beijing, and Tianjin in the north, Shanghai at the exit of the Yangtze River, and Chongqing, formerly the capital of Sichuan province and designated in 1999 as a municipality in order to serve as the administrative center for developing the west.

Natural Beauty — Guilin, Huangshan, Wuyishan, Along the Yangtze

China is full of natural beauties. Mention the beauty of nature and what conjures up one's mind are mountains and waters. The word "water" in Chinese is used to follow and pair off with the word "mountain" to describe natural scenery. A "mountain-water painting" is a Chinese painting of nature including mountains and/or rivers, lakes, but seldom oceans. Once a Chinese friend asked me whether I have a preference for mountains or water. I thought for a while and could not answer. He said he preferred mountains. I tried to understand why. When one is at a mountain, not only does one behold beautiful sights, one is imbedded in the environment and can feel and smell. When one travels by a lake or a river, however, one gets a good view but cannot claim to have a complete experience unless one submerges oneself in the water. Men live on land and not in the water. This may be why many people prefer mountains. It is mountains that people often think about when they recall experiences from traveling to see or "absorb" the beauty of nature.

When I decided to write about the natural beauty of China, I first thought of mountains. Before visiting the mountains of China, I had been to the mountains of Switzerland several times, the mountains of Norway, and the Rocky Mountains in the United States. Each has its beauty. When I got to Guilin, I thought that its mountains were unique. When I went to Huangshan (Yellow Mountains) I was deeply impressed by what I saw and experienced, perhaps more so than when visiting all the other mountains before. I visited Wuyishan more recently, in 2000, and enjoyed my visit more than my trip to Huangshan.

Guilin

In 1980, I was one of the seven American economists to lecture on econometrics in a summer workshop in Beijing. As a part of the invitation, each lecturer was given the opportunity to select several places to visit, accompanied by a guide. Some visitors still had the notion that the guide was assigned to restrict their movements and to spread government propaganda. This might have been the case in the 1970s but was not true in the 1980s. The truth was that in the Chinese planned economy in 1980, allocation of many goods and services was not by the market. A visitor needed a guide with some government connections to buy first-class train tickets, to get a room in a hotel and to get good theater tickets, etc. Guilin was one of the places my wife and I chose to visit.

So many foreign tourists have visited Guilin that I do not need to describe it at length. President Clinton visited Guilin in 1999. He decided to stay two and half hours longer than scheduled. As a result, the reception in Hong Kong was delayed for almost three hours, with the Chief Executive and about 100 other Hong Kong dignitaries waiting in hunger. What is so interesting about Guilin?

The most memorable part of a visit to Guilin is a boat trip along the Li River, with beautiful and unusual mountains on all sides. As the trip starts one first notices the Chinese row boats going by, some occupied by fishermen. Their appearance and their style of fishing can be interesting to a foreign tourist. So are the scenes of nearby houses, farms and villages. Then the excitement of the trip intensifies. More and more mountains begin to appear. Their shapes are special, different from mountains elsewhere. The mountains seem to have shot up from the ground like a bullet, unlike other mountains that have much gentler slopes and gradual inclines. They have been captured in Chinese paintings. There are numerous such mountains of different sizes and shapes lined on both sides of the river and forming interesting compositions as groups. The compositions are determined by the viewer, depending on his good taste and ingenuity.

The boat ride along the Li River takes about two hours. Sitting on the upper deck, one can enjoy viewing each mountain with its own characteristics, or a group of mountains in a composition. Although the boat is moving slowly, there is so much to see in all directions that a viewer feels that he is missing much of the scenery because he runs out of time. He turns his head from left to right, but never fast enough to catch everything he wants to see and yet too fast to enjoy sufficiently each sight he composes in his vision camera. Before long he is disappointed as the enjoyment comes to an end when the boat reaches its destination, a small market town in 1980. The visitor sighs, not quite believing what he has just experienced. He is eager to tell his friends back home, and ask them to take a trip to Guilin.

Huangshan (Yellow Mountains)

Paula, our daughter Mei and I went to Huangshan in 1985. In the summer of 1985, after organizing and teaching a workshop in macroeconomics under the sponsorship of the State Education Commission and meeting with the Premier Zhao Ziyang, I was invited to visit a few most famous places in China. China's economy was rapidly changing to a market economy, but was much poorer than it is today. If a tourist goes to Huangshan today, there are modern hotels and a cable car to take her to the top. In 1985, there was no cable car, and we had to walk up. There was only one hotel in the most desired area on top of one of the mountains. Rooms in that hotel were very difficult to get. People slept on the hallways of the hotel. All floor space was in fact used up. When we went out of our room to use the washroom outside the hotel building, we literally had to step across these tourists who were fortunate enough to have a hotel floor to sleep on. Without good government connections, we could not have gotten our rooms.

A car took us to a parking area about one third of the way up the top, as the farthest that it could go. We then walked up a path moderately steep at some points. It took us almost half a day to walk up this rocky path, while workers carrying goods to the top could make two round trips a day. Along the way, we looked around and sometimes stopped briefly to look down from the mountain slope. Looking around we marveled at the trees in the mountain. The pine trees are particularly interesting. They have unusual shapes and the colors are of different grades of brown and green. The shapes show different characteristics, like a human body that can bend in different ways. Bent in a one way, a tree can look very strong, just like a strong man. The dark green gives a feeling of serenity. These trees are a favorite subject for Chinese painters, as well as the rest of Huangshan. One can enjoy both the paintings and the scenery better if one studies both. I display on the next page a painting of Huangshan. Besides the famous pine trees, there are many other kinds of trees and plants for a botanist to appreciate. When we reached the top eventually, we were convinced that Huangshan is indeed one of the most beautiful mountains. Huangshan can be translated into Yellow Mountain or Yellow Mountains in English since a noun in Chinese like "shan" can be singular or plural. If one cares to speculate why this is the case, perhaps the Chinese think more about the nature or characteristics of things and less about quantity. "Shan" means mountain. It matters less whether there is one or (there are) two. (The Chinese do not distinguish a verb as being singular or plural either. The meaning of a verb is clear without such a distinction.) In the Chinese way of thinking Huangshan is this "shan" that we can enjoy visiting without thinking about whether it is one, two or three.

"Wen Shu Yuan" — a Painting of Huangshan by renowned artist Zhang Daqian
(Painting courtesy of M K Lau Collection Limited)

Indeed there are several mountains in the Huangshan area. I do not recall how many we went to. They are connected, one leading to another. Besides the special pine trees along the slopes, the unusual features are the rocks of the mountain and the rapidly changing climatic conditions. The mood of a visitor changes with the light, the clouds, the mist, the air as well as the different views of the trees, the rocks and the mountains from different perspectives. The rocks are really unusual. They are rough looking and show strong characters. A person can be inspired and feel strong by looking at them. Their shapes are sharp and angular, whereas the rocks of the mountains in Guilin are soft and smooth by comparison. Some mountains in Switzerland are rocky too, but more like very large pieces of rocks. In Huangshan the rocks are more individualized and smaller. Each is distinct and shows its own character.

The view is different when it is sunny, cloudy, rainy, or misty. It also varies with the way the sun shines in the course of the day, with how the clouds are formed, with the degree of rainfall, and with how misty it is. Huangshan is distinguished by its variety and many changes in appearance. In terms of variety, the trees, the rocks and the climate all have a great deal to offer. In terms of changes in appearance, the sunlight, the clouds and the mist move with the mountain in the background, prompting it to take on ever-changing looks. The grotesque rocks and the unusual trees are a part of the scenery that changes. It is easy to appreciate why there was a famous school of paintings in the 17th century that was founded by painting the scenery of Huangshan. After my visit I told my friends that if there were only one place to visit in China for beautiful and spectacular scenery, it would be Huangshan. I had heard the same from friends before my visit.

Wuyishan

I visited Wuyishan in the summer of 2000, 20 years after I had visited Guilin. My host was also the Chinese Academy of Social

Science as before. In 1980, there were seven economists lecturing on econometrics in Beijing with the Academy as host. In 2000 our host organization decided to invite all seven of us to Beijing again for the 20th anniversary of our first visit in the form of a conference in econometrics. All seven accepted and attended the conference. In 1980, no one in China knew much about econometrics, or at least no one had learned it in China or taught it. When the field was developed in the United States in the early 1950s, mainly in the University of Chicago where I studied, China began closing its door to the Western world. In 1980 the door was reopened and we were the first group invited to teach economics, in the field of econometrics that was considered to be ideologically neutral in our host country. In 2000, we were much impressed by the growth of the field in China, as witnessed partly by the papers presented in the conference.

All of us were provided business-class tickets (costing about 8,500 US dollars) to go to the conference in Beijing. Our spouse and we stayed in five-star hotels. I wondered how the Chinese Academy of Social Science could afford to pay such expenses. The answer was that our trip was financed mainly by other organizations. Among them was the government of the Province of Fujian, west of the Taiwan Strait. The provincial government was hosting over 2,000 foreign investors and trade representatives in a huge and impressive new building in Xiamen on the coast, facing Taiwan. We were asked to be speakers in an economic forum targeted at the business people. I accepted the invitation to speak reluctantly. Our host from the Academy insisted that we must visit Wuyishan after the economic forum because it was one of the best tourist attractions in China. He turned out to be right. Visiting Wuyishan alone compensated, in fact more than compensated, the preparation of several speeches that our trip to China required.

We stopped in Xiamen for half a day just to perform our necessary official functions, including the speech at the economics forum and meetings with dignitaries from Beijing and foreign countries. Then we were immediately escorted to Wuyishan in the northwest of the Province of Fujian by government foreign-trade officials. The mayor of the county, much of the time represented by a deputy mayor, hosted us for three days. He gave us an official welcome when we first arrived, dined with us several times, and said goodbye to us when we left. (My family and I were also guests of the Chinese government while we visited Huangshan, and the mayor in the locality showed similar courtesy, as this is a common practice in China when the government plays host.)

Wuyishan combines some of the beauties of Guilin and Huangshan. Guilin has both water and mountain, and Huangshan does not. Wuyishan has a river and some of the mountains in the precinct look like the mountains of Huangshan, except that they are in smaller scales. Like Huangshan, Wuyishan embodies variety, albeit a different kind of variety.

A trip along the river in Wuyishan is very enjoyable, although not quite as exciting as looking around on the top deck of a motorboat on the Li River. Instead of a large motorboat, a tourist gets to ride on a long boat rowed by two persons, one on each end. The boat is a bit like a gondola in Venice, but it is longer and holds several more people. It is made of bamboo. Its construction requires specially treated bamboo branches and very skillful workmanship. It is a piece of artwork. Such a boat costs only about US$250 at the time. A family of two would save up enough to buy one and register it in the government tourist office. Many such boats line up in a designated location on the riverbank waiting for a government official to call them. There were nine famous inscriptions on the rocks along the route covered by a boat trip. While a tourist is admiring the beautiful mountains all around, the guide and rower in front would explain to him the writing on a rock of interest and its historical meaning, in the same way that a guide on a gondola in Venice would explain the history and significance of a special building. While the motorboat on Li River sails upstream, a rowboat here goes downstream for the convenience of the rowers. The water moves quite fast. The entire trip takes about an hour and half.

Besides seeing the mountains by boat, a tourist would go to the mountains. One favorite spot has a small pavilion on the side of a mountain. The leading Neo-Confucian scholar Zhu Xi (1130–1200) of the Song dynasty met his students in this pavilion. Zhu Xi was considered the successor of Confucius and Menzi deserving the title of Master Zhu. He extended or reinterpreted traditional Confucianism to answer questions in cosmology and metaphysics. These are topics lacking in traditional Confucianism but treated in Daoism and Buddhism, competing schools or ideas that had gained importance in China. One can imagine how the environment of the pavilion was suitable for Master Zhu to expound his teaching of the "order" or *li* as his teaching is so named. Zhu Xi realized the importance of his teaching, often comparing himself with Confucius rather than considering himself a disciple. I spent a long time looking at the pavilion from below and walking around it after I had hiked up the trail to the pavilion. I wondered what some of the scenes might have been with Master Zhu giving lectures to his students.

Instead of walking up the path to the pavilion one can follow an opposite path to a higher point with a scenic view of the mountains around. There are many things to do while one is at a mountain. One can view it from a distance or from a nearby spot below, view the surrounding mountains from any spot of the mountain, walk around different areas to see trees and plants, etc. Wuyishan is good for any of these. It is a series of mountains, each beautiful and different from the other. One can watch the river where the bamboo boats take tourists to see the mountains from below. Our time was limited since there were many other sites to visit.

One favorite site is the ruins of an old city. The city was destroyed by the army from the government in the north because the people living there were rebellious during the Han dynasty. They declared independence and the central government tried to subdue them without success for years. Although they were few in numbers, the people were well trained militarily, brave and well disciplined. When the army of the central government finally won, it decided to burn the city and killed many residents. Much of the city wall still remains. One can see the remains of the old living quarters, with parts of the rooms and even stoves. Historians have rediscovered the way people lived at the time, providing interesting stories for the tour guides to tell, although sometimes incorrectly. The guides of the Wuyishan area are well trained and quite knowledgeable about many topics of interest. Visiting that site was like visiting a museum, except that most of the objects were not well preserved. However it provides the actual environment in which the objects were actually used.

The second site that left a strong impression on me is a place for tea drinking. Fujian province is famous for its tea, as is Taiwan across the Taiwan Strait. The climate of Fujian and Taiwan are similar, and perhaps the soil as well. The Taiwan people are mostly immigrants from Fujian. One major Fujian dialect is spoken in Taiwan. As a result of a long period of economic prosperity, Taiwan has improved its tea and refined the way of tea drinking, including the chinaware for it. The site in Wuyishan has one tree on the slope of a hill about 70 meters above the bottom. The tea produced from its leaves is considered the best of its kind in China. Since there is only one such tree, the tea it produces is very expensive. The tree itself is well known. We could only admire the tree from below but did not get to taste the tea. As a consolation, our host served us the tea from another tree nearby, on the same slope. That was its "descendent", cultivated by grafting a branch from the first tree. The tea we tasted was excellent.

After the trip, I concluded that my visit to Wuyishan was more enjoyable than my visit to Huangshan. This may be due to personal circumstances. The conditions of my two visits were different. The hotel I stayed in Wuyishan was far superior. The Wuyishan area was much less crowded. Certain places in Huangshan were so congested that I could not really enjoy myself. There were not many tourists in Wuyishan. Furthermore there was the river, and many historical sites of interest, including the pavilion of Master Zhu and the ruins of the ancient city and more. Perhaps there are sites related to the

Huangshan school of painting that I missed, but philosophy and intellectual history of China may be more exciting for me than the history of a particular school of painting.

Along the Yangtze

In the summer of 1982, I visited five universities in China. Going from Wuhan to Chongqing, I took a boat with my wife and two children up the Yangtze River. At the time the boats were old and very crowded. There were three classes of passengers, the first class on the upper level with private rooms, the second class below with seats, and the third class below with the passengers sitting on the floor. Many third class passengers were peasants and workers. What impressed me most was seeing these people traveling to find work in other places. At the time a most serious economic problem in China was the lack of labor mobility under a system of central planning. The urban population needed resident permits to live in a particular city. The peasants worked in Communes and were assigned to a work team. In 1982, collective farming under the Commune system was disappearing. Farmers began to find work in nearby towns, or even in cities far away. They could also travel to sell their produce, including chickens and pigs that we saw on the boat. I witnessed how free trade and labor mobility can improve economic well being. It was an exciting experience for an economist.

There is much Chinese history along the Yangtze River. Many are most familiar with the history of the period of the Three Kingdoms because of the popular historical novel *Romance of the Three Kingdoms*. The kingdom of Wei was controlling the area surrounding the capital Xi'an of Han dynasty as its leader took over power from the Han emperor. It included Xi'an and area northwest of the basin of the Yangtze River. The kingdom of Shu occupied the western part of the river basin, including the Sichuan Province of today. The kingdom of Wu was in the east, including the area of Shanghai of today. By one famous account in the novel, Zhuge

Liang, the master strategist minister of Shu that had inferior military power, designed a plan to set fire on an entire fleet of Wei along the Yangtze River and succeeded in destroying it. He planned to send small boats to set fire on the connected warships of Wei, but he needed the help of east wind to burn all the boats and obtained the wind by appealing to god, or perhaps simply on the basis of knowledge of weather forecasting. He was the hero of the novel about the three Kingdoms and naturally succeeded in this venture. Any Chinese who has read the novel would look around the area known as Red Cliffs where this event took place. A well-known poet Su Shi in the Song period, whom I mentioned in connection with Song poetry, lamented the happenings of the Three Kingdoms in the Red Cliffs. That adds to the history along the Yangtze. I was telling our son James stories of the Three Kingdoms as we viewed the scenery from the boat, while our daughter Mei was too young to be interested.

Parts of the Yangtze River are wide. On the boat we could not see the shore in any direction. There are all kinds of fish and river creatures. In a museum in a city along the river we saw a very large turtle from the river. The color of the water is yellow, although the name Yellow River or Huanghe is reserved for the second main river north of and parallel to the Yangtze. Yellow River and Yellow Mountain are two familiar names in China. The Chinese civilization was thought to have started in areas near the Yellow River, but recent archeological discoveries suggest that other areas including areas near and even south of the Yangtze had ancient civilizations of similar accomplishments too.

The main attraction of a boat trip on the Yangtze for most tourists is the Three Gorges. The river is narrow. The surrounding mountains are steep. The water flows rapidly. The sights from the boat were remarkable. When one gets to a mountain, an attractive view is looking up from below. The taller the mountain and the steeper the slope, the more spectacular is the view. Many tourists considered the Three Gorges the most spectacular sight in China. For some reason, perhaps because of high expectations, I was not sufficiently impressed and in fact somewhat disappointed while going through the Three Gorges. Since the construction of the Three Gorges Dams the water levels are higher and the heights of the mountains seen from a boat are reduced, making the view less attractive. I have not returned to the area to observe the difference, but it is still considered a very attractive place to visit. A tourist in 2003 was most impressed by the massive constructions in connection with the Three Gorges Project.

Historical Sites

From nature I turn to human constructions. China itself is like a huge museum with sites constructed and objects accumulated over thousands of years. For presentation I have selected Beijing, the vicinity of Beijing (the Great Wall and the Ming Tombs) and Xi'an, although many other historical sites can be included. The very limited coverage is due to the availability of many books on the sites of China.

Beijing and Nearby Sites

Beijing is probably one of the cities that foreign tourists would visit in their first trip to China. It is the capital city of China with all the associated activities taking place to provide excitement. Within the city there are the Imperial Palace, museums, Tiananmen Square, the Summer Palace, the Heaven Pavilion (Tiantan) and other interesting places to visit. From the city a tourist can visit the nearby Great Wall and the Ming Tombs. One can easily spend two weeks to see these places, but unfortunately many tourists have only ten days for the entire China, and most of them would like to see at least one or perhaps two other places. They would choose Xi'an, Shanghai, Hong Kong or the natural scenery of one of the places mentioned earlier in this chapter. That leaves perhaps only three to four days in Beijing. They would rush through some of the sites in

Beijing, only to return home to tell their friends that they wish they had spent more time in this place or that.

Consider a visit to the Imperial Palace. It is a large museum. When one visits the Metropolitan Museum in New York City for two to three hours, one concentrates on one exhibit and does not try to walk through all the rooms quickly. The latter is what most tourists of the Palace Museum would do when they could allocate only three hours to the entire place. There are many structures to go through. In the Qing dynasty the imperial family lived in the Palace where the emperor attended to state affairs. The large imperial family and their many attendants needed much space and many buildings. The administration of the affairs of the state also required space. Viewed from the south, there is one structure near the southern entrance followed by several structures leading north and eventually to the building where the emperor received his ministers or deserving subjects. A tourist can start from the southern entrance and walk northward to experience what it would be like to visit the emperor. Besides the buildings that are lined up from south to north, there are buildings on both sides. These buildings are also interesting to visit. Going northward, the tourist will go out the northern entrance, where she and her friends can find a taxicab to go to the next site or to a restaurant.

There are many things to see in and around the Imperial Palace. One is the entrance from the South Gate. The palace is surrounded by high walls. It is interesting to go up to the platform of the wall of the South Gate and catch the grand view of the famous Tiananmen Square, the same view that Chairman Mao had on October 1, 1949 when he announced the founding of the People's Republic of China. On that day there was a huge crowd of tens of thousands of people listening to him announcing the founding of the PRC and celebrating this great historical event together. Leaving the entrance of the South Gate, one can start walking northward from building to building. The architecture of each building is representative of one form of Chinese imperial architecture. There are steps to walk up to the entrance, with interesting decorations on the railings on both sides. One will notice special features of the entrance, the hall, the ceiling, the walls, the pillars and the exhibits inside each building. There is a long piece of wood guarding the entrance that one needs to cross in order to enter. I can remember old family buildings where the entrance had such a guard, though not as high as those in the buildings of the Imperial Palace. I was told that one of its functions was to prevent rainwater from flooding into the building. In a building for the use of the emperor and his family or his ministers, people should not enter so easily without obstruction and should pause to pay respect and attention. On top of the entrance is a sign giving the name of the building. Sometimes the name was written both in Han Chinese and in the Manchu language, as the Qing emperors were Manchus. The ceiling is tall, befitting a building in a palace. There are engravings to look at. What is inside each building varies. There may be furniture that was actually used by the previous occupants, or exhibits of different kinds placed there by the administrators of the current Palace Museum, as the Imperial Palace is now used as a museum.

Concerning exhibits, there is so much to talk about but not sufficient space here. I was particularly interested in the calligraphy and paintings in some of the buildings. In the section on calligraphy and painting in Chapter 2, I mentioned some of the features of Chinese calligraphy that may help one appreciate it. As in music appreciation one's own involvement and experience add to the enjoyment. Besides calligraphy and paintings a visitor can enjoy many other treasures from an imperial palace. Although the government of the Republic of China moved some of the best to Taiwan, now being exhibited in the Palace Museum in Taipei, many new pieces have been collected from all over China and added to the collection in the Palace Museum in Beijing. Among the treasures that a visitor would notice are jade pieces, clothing, and objects that the imperial family used daily.

The Summer Palace

As its name suggests, the imperial family used the Summer Palace during the summer. There is a lake to make the place cool. Tourists are often guided to view a large boat built of marble. The boat has two stories. From my memory, it is about 100 feet long and 40 feet wide. A guide would explain that the Emperor Dowager in late Qing dynasty wasted the treasure of the government to build such a boat while the country was being defeated by one foreign imperial power after another. There is no reason to believe that China lost the wars because of the construction of this boat, as some guides would say. If the Qing government had been more competent, China would have been able to institute reform for modernization and to face the foreign powers diplomatically and militarily. Some luxury of the imperial government was not the cause of China's problem. In any case the boat is for the present generation and future generations to enjoy. Besides this stationary boat, there are boats on the lake with passengers on them. The scenery around the lake is quite beautiful.

There are many buildings around the lake. One was used for the summer econometric workshop in 1980 that I have mentioned. It was the best lecture hall that our host of the Chinese Academy of Social Science could provide at the time to hold a large class of about 100. Since a historical building was constructed without air-conditioning, a few electric fans were used to cool the room filled with so many persons, sitting on small upright chairs close to one another. As lecturers we worked hard in the hot weather and could not pay attention to enjoy the beautiful view outside. Among the more interesting structures in the Summer Palace is a long corridor which provides people with a shade while the weather is hot and a shelter when it rains. One can imagine historical figures conversing about important affairs of the states as they walked through this corridor. One Chinese movie had a scene of Yuan Shikai, the first President of the Republic of China, pondering along the corridor to decide on what to do. Yuan had lost the support of his ministers and members of the parliament in his attempt to become an emperor in the fifth year of the Republic. One can also imagine the Empress Dowager walking along that corridor to devise plans to counter armies from eight foreign countries which were invading Beijing in reaction to the damage to their citizens in China during the Boxer Rebellion in 1901.

Looking up from the corridor, a visitor can see a building high up on the side of a hill. Inside that building is a well-known restaurant. It has been advertised that it serves the same dinner that was served to the emperor. It does offer a great variety of dishes that are supposed to be the same as what the emperor consumed. One hundred dishes were served in one meal to the emperor or the Empress Dowager. She would sample only a few that seemed appetizing while leaving the rest untouched. Most tourists presumably will taste all the dishes that they order from the emperor's menu. Unlike the emperor they have to pay for the dishes. I first tasted some of the dishes in 1980 and was not impressed by the quality, considering that they were supposed to be good enough to serve to the emperor. I have been back there several times since. The food each time was better than the previous time, as a sign of economic progress of China. One day may come when the food will be better than what the Qing emperor had, if there is sufficient progress in the culinary skills. Some say that because of economic progress the best tea served in Taiwan today is better than the tea previously available in the island or in Fujian province.

Tiantan (Heaven Pavilion)

A favorite tourist site is a large and colorful structure known as Tiantan (Heaven Pavilion). In important occasions the Chinese needed a place to worship and to thank heaven for the good fortune. In a festival after harvest, they would thank heaven for providing good weather for growing and harvesting the crops. In occasions marking significant events of the dynasty, imperial rulers would thank heaven for the good fortune bestowed on them.

Tiantan was the place for the imperial rulers of the Ming and Qing dynasties to do so. It represents one form of Chinese architecture. It is built like a dome, with colorful roof tiles on top. One can visit the site to see both the architecture of the building and the whole area surrounding it. In a normal day, there are many tourists walking around to enjoy the fresh air and the view of the building from a distance, or to enjoy one another's presence.

Tiananmen Square

Located in the South of the Imperial Palace, Tiananmen Square could well be the largest public square in the world. Mao used it to make speeches to big crowds. The famous student demonstration in 1989 took place in Tiananmen Square. To celebrate the 50th anniversary of the founding of the People's Republic of China, there was a big show broadcast by all major TV channels around the world. The most impressive part of the show seemed to be the marching in unison of groups representing different segments of China. Every marcher had an identical solemn expression and turned to exactly the same direction. The steps were perfectly synchronized. The lines formed by the marchers were straight like a ruler, and had the same distance apart. A viewer of the show on TV could hardly believe that this was humanly possible. Only cartoonists in Walt Disney's studio can make a motion picture that looks like that. When I expressed admiration for the show, a friend in Princeton told me that he had marched in an important occasion in front of Tiananmen Square while he was a college student in China. Intensive training of the students to march started about half a year before the event. It was like military training, very strict and with great discipline. Hours were spent each day, like rehearsing a play by the principal actors.

The Square is a wonderful place to walk about. There are several buildings in the area that are of interest and worth visiting. The Great Hall of the People is a huge building used for government functions. There are many rooms and some rooms can seat thousands of people. It is used for government meetings and for government officials to meet foreign visitors. The Historical Museum is interesting. One exhibit shows the history of China from ancient times to the present. I have noticed a Marxian interpretation of history in the exhibit. A major theme of this interpretation is that the Chinese dynastic changes were the result of revolutions by exploited peasants. Karl Marx viewed a society as composed of social classes in conflict with one another in a "class struggle." Such an idea originated from his view of the working class being exploited by the capitalist class in 19th century England. Social changes could be achieved only by a proletarian revolution. Although such class conflicts might not have existed in China, a Marxian would interpret a change of dynasty as a revolution by an exploited class. Since industrial workers did not exist in China and only peasants were poor, they had to be viewed as the exploited. Hence such wars were said to be peasant revolutions. A more natural interpretation is that as a dynasty declined the ruling emperor and his ministers did not function properly. They lost the mandate of Heaven. Some revolutionaries organized themselves to overthrow the existing ruler. Most of the people actually engaged in fighting had to be peasants. The scholars were not sufficient in number and were not interested in or able to fight. This was the case in the Communist revolution led by Mao Zedong, an intellectual who once worked in the library of Peking University. His armies were made up mainly of peasants. The army of Chiang Kai-shek during the Northern Expedition to unify China consisted mainly of peasants also. It was often the smart leaders who wanted to utilize the peasants to fight for their political self-interests, and possibly for the interest of China as well. In February 2003 the History Museum was converted into the National Museum which includes a wider range of exhibits including science and technology that China has invented or developed.

There are so many interesting things to see and places to visit in Beijing that I cannot detail them here. There is a park north of the Imperial Palace with beautiful trees and a lake for tourists to row boats. There are Buddhist temples, gardens, universities, old streets and alleys, a small section of the old city wall (most of which was torn down for the sake of widening the roads and to the regret of many citizens), and shops for antiques and paintings, not to mention very good restaurants.

Sites near Beijing

The Great Wall is a must for tourists. An air-conditioned bus can take a visitor there in about an hour and half from the city. One can walk around to admire this great historical construction and walk up a part of the wall. I have found the slope of a certain section open to tourists to be quite steep, more so than one can expect from viewing it from a distance. Inspecting the steps and the walls one wonders how such difficult and massive work in the construction could be done by workers hundreds of years ago. In fact, when the First Emperor of Qin built and connected parts of the Great Wall, workers were recruited to work for years without being able to return home. Such an undertaking was inhuman from our viewpoint of today, but not uncommon in slave societies. The Great Wall was constructed in several dynasties, and was over 1,000 miles long. Much of it has been destroyed. One section near Beijing has been restored to preserve history and for the benefit of the tourists.

Because of geographical convenience the same bus would probably pass by the Ming Tombs. The Ming Emperors, like emperors of other dynasties, wanted to be buried in a large and elaborately constructed tomb. The dead needed comfort in their afterlife. Not only their physical belongings but also the people close to them were buried with them. Considered as living quarters the size of a tomb had to be large. Its contents had to be worthy for the occupant, and thus became interesting to the tourists. Its surrounding had to be suitable for an emperor, alive or dead. Since many emperors of different generations would wish to live in the same area, a large space had to be selected to house all of them. That is why the Ming Tombs, build to house several Ming emperors and close relatives, were found in one large area. Each tomb had to face the right direction and properly situated just as a carefully designed house of today. It is considered desirable to have mountains on both sides, for the sake of protection, and to have the tomb facing south, perhaps for protection from the cold wind from the north. If the person residing in the tomb lives in comfort, his offspring will prosper and also live in comfort.

Xi'an

Xi'an is best known as the site of the tomb of the Qin Emperor. From what I have just described about the nature and function of a tomb, one can understand why the Qin Emperor wanted such a large and elaborate tomb for himself. The tomb is one and half kilometers in diameter. It is under and covered by a low and very gently sloping mountain. Most of it has not been excavated. The part open to the tourists is the entrance to an underground palace that needed protection by several thousand soldiers. Some 2,000 terracotta soldiers have been dug up and restored. The scale of the tomb is really impressive considering that it was built over 2,000 years ago. The quality of the work is admirable as shown in the facial expression of each warrior. Each represents a different person. It is difficult to find such good sculpture produced in such a grand scale. It must have been extracting for the Qing sculptors to produce so many warriors of exact measurements, shapes and specified faces and facial expressions. There are also horses and horse carriages made with the same quality to accompany the soldiers. One can only imagine what might be inside the tomb-palace for the soldiers we see are only a small part of the palace at its entrance.

The Xi'an Museum is nearby. It is a historical museum housing many of the objects of the time. I was impressed by the ammunitions of the Qin period exhibited there. It required an advanced technology to produce them. One can appreciate why Qin succeeded in conquering the six other strong states to unify China.

The military power of Qin might be compared to the military power of Germany in the Second World War in conquering a number of European nations, at least for a time. The German guns, tanks, warships, and submarines were supposed to be technologically superior at the time. Some found their way to museums also.

Xi'an itself is known as a historical city. It was the capital of Zhou dynasty and was called Changan. "Chang" means long, extended or lasting, and "an" means "peace." That seems to be a suitable name for a capital. During the later part of the Zhou dynasty, the capital was moved eastward to Loyang (called Louyi at the time). Historians call the early period West-Zhou and the later period East-Zhou, referring to the location of its capital. Changan became Xi'an, where "xi" means west. A few sections of the ancient city remain. As a part of modern Chinese history, it is the site of the famous Xi'an Incident in 1936 when Chiang Kai-shek was captured by one of his generals in Xi'an and forced to make peace with the Communists and to fight the Japanese invaders together. This incident could have changed the course of history, by preventing Chiang from defeating the Communists. One can only speculate what would have happened without this incident.

Between the time of Zhou dynasty and the Xi'an Incident of 1936, Xi'an was the capital of Tang dynasty when great poetry flourished. The poet Bai Juyi lamented the love affair of Tang Emperor Ming with his concubine that took place in Xi'an. A part of the poem can be literally translated as follows, "In a cold Spring day the emperor allowed her to bathe in the Huaqing Pond [near the location where Chiang was captured]. The soothing water from the hot spring washed her saturated skin. The attendants lifted up the bathing beauty as she was lacking in strength. This was when love was first bestowed upon." When a tourist visits this site with a pond and a hill beside it, she will be told that the Tang beauty bathed here and Chiang was captured after trying to escape by running up the hill. She can also enjoy bathing with the same hot spring water in one of the rooms provided for tourists.

US-China Relations

I have presented China in its many dimensions. This background knowledge helps in placing US-China relation in a proper perspective. To set the stage I will first address the position of the United States as the dominant world power. I will then discuss the basis of US-China relation, and this relation in the context of the power structure of nations in East Asia. Some people consider China a threat to the United States, but I will discuss possible advantages in considering China as a strategic partner, as former President Clinton suggested and current President Bush has come to realize.

The United States as a World Power before and after 9/11, 2001

For four and half decades between the end of the Second World War and the fall of the Berlin Wall in 1991, world peace was maintained by the balance of power of the United States and the Soviet Union. After the Cold War ended, world peace and security has been and will be maintained by the dominance of the United States. The United States is the most powerful country in the world. In some respects its military power may even surpass the rest of the world combined. This is true in terms of the power of its nuclear weapons. As the most powerful nation, the United States has an important role in maintaining world peace and security. How the United States exercises its role as the dominant world power determines the peace and the security of the world to a large extent.

The role of the United States as the world leader has changed significantly after the tragic event of 9/11, 2001. It has waged a major war against terrorism for the sake of the security of its people at home. In doing so it has extended its role as a world leader. In the process of fighting world terrorism, the United States is extending its power by the possible use of preemptive strikes if a threat is found. To use preemptive strikes is a new concept not used by the United States or any post-Second World War world power before 9/11. Terrorists can be found anywhere and any country having dangerous military weapons can harbor terrorists and thus threaten the security at home. The United States, therefore, has found itself involved in more conflicts than before, in Afghanistan, in Iraq, and in North Korea as of the time this book is written in the spring of 2003. Although no other nation is in a position to threaten the United States, the help and cooperation of other nations are needed more than before in order for the Unites States to maintain its world leadership and to fight terrorism. In February 2003, the United States had difficulty in getting the support of major nations including China, France, Germany and Russia to wage a war against Iraq. To maintain a leadership role in its increased involvement in world affairs, the United States needs the support of other major nations including China.

9 The Basis of US-China Relations

At the end of Second World War, the United States became a super power. Most of the post Second World War period was dominated by the rivalry between the US and the Soviet Union. After the collapse of the Berlin Wall and the beginning of the disintegration of world communism, the threat and rivalry from the Soviet Union disappeared. Some people in the United States still have the mentality of facing a major enemy. To them, China can easily be considered as Soviet Union's replacement. As a superpower the US naturally desires to maintain its leadership position. In the meantime China has emerged as a major world power, though nowhere as strong as the United States from the military viewpoint. Some Americans may sense a certain degree of rivalry between the two countries.

Should the US regard China as a friend or an adversary? Historically there was a special friendship between the US and China. Americans helped China in the establishment of modern educational institutions and hospitals. The two countries were allies during the Second World War. To the extent that the US is unfriendly to China, it is mainly because China is ruled by a communist party. Communism was regarded as a threat to world peace and security after the Second World War. It has taken some time for people to realize that after the political and economic transformation of the former Soviet Union and socialist Eastern European countries, the threat of world communism no longer exists. Only a few countries remain ruled by a communist party. China and Vietnam in particular have changed their economic and social system and are no threat to world peace.

There is a distinction between a country that has a communist party in power and a country that practices orthodox communism. Communism in China is the name of a party that is practicing the ideas of a market economy, which is the basis of capitalism. If Deng Xiaoping had had the name of the Communist Party changed when he decided to divert the course from central planning toward a market economy, the US would view China as a friend. Such a move, which never occurred to Deng, would have eroded the support of the Party members for economic reform. We need to understand the Chinese government by its actions instead of its name, as we were accustomed to interpret it. This understanding cannot come about if we start with a perceived notion that the Chinese Communists are bad, and refuse to change our view on the basis of new evidence. Like any enduring institution, the Chinese Communist Party adjusts itself to changing environment in its ideas and policies. By observing its policies to institute market reform measures, to open China's door to foreign investment and foreign ideas, to change its education system and to allow freedom of movement and expression to its citizens — all being popular policies in China — one can conclude that its members and Chinese government officials are rational, intelligent and pragmatic in their attempt to modernize China. It would be unwise for them to adhere to outdated ideological ideas rather than to practice the best that is available. Whatever the merits and shortcomings of the Chinese government, China is a country made up of its people with a strong cultural tradition and much good will. Understanding the Chinese people and the Chinese government will form the basis of a sound US-China relation.

US-China Relation in the Power Structure of East Asia

The strategic relation between US and China can be understood by considering the power structure of the nations in East Asia. Both countries have a keen interest in this region for geographical reasons. The United States is a most important and powerful player. Its important role began in 1945 with its victory over Japan at the end of the Second World War. Without the intervention of the United States, Japan would probably have dominated most of East Asia in the name of "Co-prosperity for the Great East Asia." Japan started the war with China in 1937, as the first and most important step to conquer or at least to control the entire region. The slogan of "Co-prosperity" was used to appeal to the Asians to free themselves from the occupation by Europeans in Burma, India, Indochina, Indonesia, Malaysia and the Philippines. Japan wanted to take the place of the Europeans. To attack Pearl Harbor was a part of this grand design. When Japan was defeated in 1945, the United States was the savior of Asia and took over the leadership role from Japan. The US occupied Japan and changed its government structure. Japan became subservient to the United States.

In the meantime, major threats to US power in this region could come from China and the Soviet Union. Both were allies of the

United States during Second World War, but soon became its enemies. The world power struggle was between the United States and the Soviet Union, with much of the conflicts taking place in Europe. Eastern European countries became members of the Soviet Bloc and the Western European countries joined the United States in forming the North-Atlantic Treaty Organization (NATO). The US Soviet conflict extended to Asia as well. It was unfortunate for the United States (and for me personally as a foreign student from China) that the Communists took over China in 1949. The United States considered China a part of the Soviet Bloc. The Cold War started. It was a war between two great powers, sometimes labeled as between two ideologies, Communism and Capitalism or Democracy. Communism represented both an economic system and a political system. It took two words — capitalism and democracy — to balance it from the other side. No matter whether the Cold War was viewed as a political power struggle or an ideological conflict, peace and political stability in the world including East Asia depended on the outcome of this conflict.

In East Asia during the Cold War, Japan was not a major power. The three major players were the US, Soviet Union and China from 1949 up to 1991, when the Soviet Union began to break up. To contain Communism or the Soviet influence, frequently treated as the same although sometimes incorrectly, the United States went to war twice, once in Korea in 1950–1 and once in Vietnam in the 1960s. During the Korean War, US led a military force authorized by the United Nations. China fought on the opposite side of the Korean War and was identified as an enemy. The Vietnam War was fought by the United States alone, leading to very serious social disturbances in the country. Eventually the US made friend with the victorious communist government in Vietnam and it has endorsed a market economic system following the lead of the Communist government in China. The current friendly policy toward Vietnam demonstrates that the US government does not consider every communist government a threat. This point should be kept in mind in the design of a suitable policy toward China. In the meantime,

North Korea, declaring its intention to build nuclear weapons as of the spring of 2003, poses a very serious threat to the United States and the region. China is being relied upon to negotiate with North Korea in order to control the spread of nuclear weapons.

The situation in East Asia today is characterized by the absence of conflicts among the four most powerful countries, Russia, China, Japan and the United States. Possible wars and instability can also come from actions of smaller countries like North Korea. Russia is not likely to seek expansion. Neither is China. Historically, China, at least under the rule of the Han Chinese, was less interested in territorial expansion than in having foreign countries pay tribute to the emperor. It was content to defend its own territory against invasions from outside. It received tributes from neighboring countries, but did not occupy them. Today the Chinese government has no interest in territorial expansion. It spends a small amount on defense, amounting to only 2 percent of GNP, as compared with about 5 percent for the US. It realizes that its own interest is better served by concentrating on improving the economic well-being of the Chinese people. War would be costly, unpopular and risky if not successful. The costs of military expansion outweigh the benefits for the Chinese government. There is nothing to gain by occupying the territory of a neighboring country. (Taiwan is considered a part of China, and its case will be discussed below.) Hence China is not a threat to the region. Japan is economically strong but militarily weak. The only remaining powerful country of the four is the United States, which has no intention to take over territories in East Asia.

If none of the four powers in the region wishes to expand, peace and stability of the region can be sustained by their mutual cooperation. The above analysis of the power structure in East Asia is valid no matter what the outcome of the current threat of North Korea's nuclear weapon development will turn out to be. To maintain political stability in the region, the best policy is for the four powers to cooperate to deal with whatever threats that may arise. I used the term "power structure" in East Asia. Political scientists often think of power politics in international relations in terms of the "balance of power." That term applies when the major powers have conflicting interests, possibly in territorial expansion, and stability is maintained by the balance of the power of one strong country against another. In the current situation in East Asia, military expansion by the major powers is not a problem. The term "power structure" seems more appropriate. Given the structure the cooperation of the major powers is necessary to prevent the spread of nuclear weapons. In particular the cooperation of China and the United States is crucial.

Possible Conflict with China over Taiwan

One possible source of conflict between the United States and China is their relations with Taiwan. While China claims Taiwan to be a part of China, the United States would seriously object if China were to try to take over Taiwan by military force. There are several reasons why it is unlikely for China to use military force to take over Taiwan. First, the Chinese government is preoccupied with economic and political modernization in the Mainland and cannot afford to waste energy to invade Taiwan. Second, invasion is risky since Taiwan has strong naval and air power to defend itself. The risk increases if the United States gives Taiwan additional military support. Failure in a military attack has serious consequences for the Chinese government in its effort to maintain political stability internally. Third, even if military invasion were to succeed in conquering Taiwan, the Chinese government would lose the support of the Taiwan people and would find it difficult, if not impossible, to rule Taiwan. Fourth, the military act would alienate the world community, hurting China's foreign investment and its international status.

Chinese leaders and government officials have proclaimed repeatedly that Taiwan is a part of China and that any sign of Taiwan declaring its independence will not be tolerated and, if necessary, will be dealt with by force. Such statements are needed to satisfy the desire of the Chinese people as they consider Taiwan a part of China. The government would lose their support if it were to give up sovereignty over Taiwan. It has even moved troops along the coast opposite Taiwan as a military threat, mainly to increase its bargaining power when negotiating with Taiwan on the issue of political integration. Short of military conflicts, it is possible for the Chinese government to send rockets near Taiwan as it did before. It may even impose blockade in certain areas to destabilize the Taiwanese economy if Taiwan's independence is declared in a form unacceptable to the Chinese government.

To the Chinese government, sovereignty over Taiwan is important, but sovereignty does not mean military takeover. This point is clear since the Chinese government has offered the Taiwan government the right to rule as it does today and to keep its own military force, as long as Taiwan becomes nominally a part of China in some acceptable manner. Thus if the Taiwan government admits being a part of China, everything else can remain the same as it is. This shows that the Chinese government has no intention to take over Taiwan by occupying it, or sending someone from China or even appointing someone from Taiwan to govern it. It only wants Taiwan to recognize the sovereignty of China and not to declare independence. If so, conflict between the United States and China concerning Taiwan is manageable. The United States does not want China to use military force to take over Taiwan. China will not in fact use military force. The only concern is the possible declaration of independence by the government of Taiwan, and the United States has discouraged this from happening.

China Not a Threat to the United States

China cannot be a military threat to the United States. It has neither the military power nor the intention to do so. The military power of the United States is many times stronger than that of China. China has no desire to be a military threat. The Chinese government is concerned with developing the economy and

Knowing China

preserving political stability and social order within the country. It has no intention of trying to expand its territory by going to war. The case of Taiwan is an exception, but military conflict over Taiwan is unlikely, as I have just discussed. If we are concerned with possible conflict with China on issues other than Taiwan, the United States as the stronger power will be able to prevent it.

Economic Competition from China

China can be a threat to the economic dominance of the United States if we define "a threat" to mean an increase in the relative economic power of China as compared with that of the United States. In Chapter 3, I have made a projection that by the year 2020 the total output of China in terms of purchasing power would equal or exceed that of the United States. The rise of the economic power of China can be threatening to the United States' economy in one important respect. Since China has high-quality and low-cost labor, many manufacturing firms from the United States and other developed economies have moved, and are moving, to China. This decreases the demand for the services from similar workers in the United States and would tend to lower their wages and reduce the employment of such workers in the United States. This tendency is unavoidable. The solution, to be achieved by market forces, is for the United States to shift its production from such manufacturing industries to some selected high-tech industries or service industries that the United States is better suited to develop than China. Historically such shifts in production have occurred in the United States to prevent the overall rate of unemployment to increase in the long run. In the short run, however, the workers displaced, some of whom are suffering a great deal, had to face painful adjustment problems.

Other things being equal, moving one factory from the United States to take advantage of the low-cost labor in China will lead to a higher national income for the United States as a whole but a lower employment and lower wage for the workers. When physical capital is moved with the factory to China, there will be less capital and hence reduced total output in United States. But the capital that is moved will earn more in China to compensate for the loss of output in the United States, otherwise the move will not be made. This leads to a net increase in the US national income. As factories are moved to China, while the United States gains in total national income or output, wages and employment of the workers in these and similar factories in the United States will be reduced. The people, including workers, owning stocks of the companies that move their factories to China will gain.

In the above analysis I have not considered other things that may happen. Competition from low-cost labor in China will provide incentives for US workers to improve their skills to find new jobs and for US entrepreneurs to develop new products or services to employ the labor now available. This is a part of the economic globalization process. I have discussed its impact on China in providing foreign competition to the Chinese state enterprises and commercial banks, as China has become a member of the WTO. The United States has an abundance of capital relative to labor, while China has an abundance of labor relative to capital. As capital moves from the United States to China, it will lower the return to capital in China and lower the wage rate in the United States, but it will raise the wage of the Chinese workers and raise the return to American capital. Both economies will have to find adjustments to weather the impact. In the long run both countries will be better off as their national incomes will increase at a faster rate as a result of economic globalization.

China's economic expansion has several favorable effects for the United States. First, as we have just pointed out, China provides investment opportunities for US investors. US corporations setting up factories in China can increase their profits which are good for their stockholders and for raising total national income. Second, China provides a large market for goods produced in the United States and helps to increase employment in the industries producing such goods. Third, China produces a large number of inexpensive and high-quality consumer goods being exported to the United States to benefit the American consumers. Economic cooperation with China is therefore beneficial to the United States and to China as well.

US-China Partnership

Whether China is a partner of US is mainly for the United States to decide. Both the Chinese government and the Chinese people desire to be friendly with the United States as they have expressed in numerous occasions. The US attitude toward China has been somewhat mixed. At times it has treated China as a partner, and at other times, as a competitor. President Clinton realized the importance of China's cooperation for the United States to maintain its world leadership. He carried out a policy of treating China as a "strategic partner." At the beginning of his administration President Bush changed this policy. Secretary of State Colin Powell in his confirmation hearing at the US Senate stated openly that "A strategic partner China is not." Less than a year later the Bush administration realized that it was important to treat China as a friend and reversed the previous policy. In fighting world terrorism the United States needs the support of China and other nations, as the Bush administration recognizes. United States and China are partners in this effort. Both the Clinton and the Bush administrations have succeeded in making China a partner once they tried.

The case for establishing a strong partnership with China is simple and obvious. The United States wishes to assert world leadership. China is a strong economic and political power, but not necessarily a military power for the United States to contend with. The role of the US as a world leader can be strengthened with the support and cooperation of China.

What are the possible exceptions to the above simple and obvious proposition? First, the US and China may have conflicting interests and can get into each other's way. If such a situation arises, it is still better to negotiate with a friend than with an enemy. A friend is more willing to compromise because he desires to preserve a mutually beneficial long-term relationship. Conflicts between enemies can lead to wars. Thus even if conflict of interest may exist, it is still desirable for the United States and China to be partners. A second possible reason rejecting this proposition is that China does not wish to be a partner of the United States, but China has expressed a strong desire to be a friend of the United States and has not rejected any gesture of friendship. Even if the friendly intention of the Chinese government is in doubt, the better policy is to treat China as a partner and observe whether the policy will bear fruits.

The benefits of economic cooperation between the two countries have been pointed out in the last section. US consumers have enjoyed good-quality and low-price products made in China. US investors have made profits by investing in China. US exporters have taken advantage of the large Chinese market, which is becoming even larger. As the US is a champion of the economic globalization process, China's membership in the WTO is good for economic development in China and elsewhere in the world. The benefits of political cooperation between the two countries have yet to be more fully realized, but the potential benefits are clear.

Peace and political stability in Asia depend on cooperation among China, India, Japan, Pakistan, Russia and the United States (listed in alphabetical order). Since there is unresolved conflict between India and·Pakistan, it is important for the remaining powerful countries to resolve such a conflict if it occurs. There is a threat of nuclear weapon development in North Korea. Cooperation between the United States and China is needed to deal with this problem. Being a major world power, China also plays a role in maintaining political stability in the rest of the world, including the situations in Iraq and Iran, the conflict between Israel and the Palestinians, and wars in Africa. China is a permanent member of the Security Council of the United Nations. In this position, its cooperation with the United States can help advance the efforts of the United States in preserving world peace through the UN. World peace and political stability can be enhanced by a strong partnership between the United States and China.

In spite of its ups and downs in the past, US-China relation has improved a great deal since 9/11, 2001 and is likely to remain on a friendly basis. With fighting world terrorism as the main objective of its foreign policy, the United States needs the support of China. China has provided this in obtaining the UN resolution on inspection of possible chemical, biological and nuclear weapons in Iraq and in finding a non-military solution for the nuclear threat from North Korea. The US government realizes that a strong partnership with China will strengthen the role of the United States as the dominant power in fighting terrorism and in maintaining peace and security in the world. This realization is enunciated by Secretary of State Colin Powell at a news conference during his visit to Beijing at the end of February 2003. The February 28 issue of *South China Morning Post*, Hong Kong's major English language newspaper, quoted Secretary Powell's remarks as follows:

> "America's relations with China have moved to a new dimension. In addition to three meetings in 18 months, Presidents George W. Bush and Jiang Zemin have had frequent phone calls and I meet my counterpart, Foreign Minister Tang Jiaxuan, almost every other week. In between, we communicate by phone on a regular basis. The US and China are now addressing … issues of worldwide concern, not just to us bilaterally, but issues that affect the entire world.

> "As a fellow permanent member of the United Nations Security Council, the US works closely with our Chinese colleagues to ensure … that Iraq cannot continue to threaten international peace and security…

"America also shares the goal of a nuclear weapons-free Korean peninsular. The US appreciates China's consistent message to the North Koreans…

"China is certainly doing its part to counter terrorism, and we are pleased with the level of cooperation…

"Human rights and religious freedom are another key area of our bilateral relationship. We are a little concerned that, after a year of promising steps in this area and a very productive US-China human rights dialogue last December, we have seen some setbacks on human rights… The US has been deeply concerned by the execution of a prominent Tibetan, the detention of more than a dozen democracy activists and the continuation of a pattern of inconsistent and irregular legal and judicial procedures. Our goal is to turn human rights into a positive element in our relationship…

"The growing cooperation between the US and China enhances both our nations, helps stabilize the region and benefits the world."

In this book I have tried to introduce China to the outside world and especially to American readers, and to call attention to the emergence of China in the world scene. Knowing China can help promote the cooperation between the people and governments of the United States and China, as well as peace and security in the world.

Bibliography

Allen, Franklin, Jun Qian and Meijun Qian. "Law, Finance, and Economic Growth in China." Pennsylvania: Finance Department, The Wharton School, University of Pennsylvania, November 2002.

Annals of Mr. Liang Yansum of Sanshiu, Volumes 1 and 2 (in Chinese). Hong Kong, private publication, 1939. Reissued as a monograph in the "Modern Chinese History Series," Taipei: Wenxing Book Company, 1962.

Au, Ada. *Do Women Hold Up Half the Sky? An Examination of the Gender Income Differential in Urban China between 1986 and 1992.* Princeton: Economics Department, Princeton University, 2000.

Buck, John L. *Chinese Farm Economy: A Study of 2,866 Farms in Seventeen Localities and Seven Provinces in China.* Chicago: University of Chicago Press, 1930.

Butterfield, Fox. *China: Alive in the Bitter Sea.* New York: Times Books, 1982.

Chan, Wingsit. *Source Book in Chinese Philosophy.* Princeton: Princeton University Press, 1963.

Chow, Gregory C. *The Chinese Economy.* New York: Harper and Row, 1985; second edition. Singapore: World Scientific Publishing Co., 1987.

Chow, Gregory C. *Understanding China's Economy.* Singapore: World Scientific Publishing Co., 1994.

Chow, Gregory C. "Challenges of China's Economic Institutions for Economic Theory," *American Economic Review*, vol. 87, no. 2 (May 1997), pp. 321–327.

Chow, Gregory C. *China's Economic Transformation*. Oxford: Blackwell Publishers, 2002.

Fong, Wen C. *Beyond Representation: Chinese Painting and Calligraphy 8th–14th Century*. New York: The Metropolitan Museum; New Haven: Yale University Press, 1992.

Fong, Wen C. and James C. Y. Watt. *Possessing the Past: Treasures from the National Palace Museum, Taipei*. New York: The Metropolitan Museum; Taipei: National Palace Museum, 1996.

Harris, Jr. Robert E. and Wen C. Fong. *The Embodied Image: Chinese Calligraphy from the John B. Elliott Collection*. Princeton: The Art Museum, Princeton University Press, 1999.

Hightower, James and Florence Chia-Ying Yeh. *Studies in Chinese Poetry*. Cambridge: Harvard University Press, 1998.

Huang, Kerson. *I Ching: The Oracle*. Singapore: World Scientific Publishing Company, 1984.

Hughes, Neil C. *China's Economic Challenge: Smashing the Iron Rice Bowl*. Armonk: M. E. Sharp, 2002.

Menzies, Gavin. *1421: The Year the Chinese Discovered the World*. London: Bantam Press, 2003.

Needham, Joseph *et al*. *Science and Civilization in China*. 7 vols. Cambridge: Cambridge University Press, 1956.

Office of the United Nations High Commissioner for Human Rights. *Annual Report 2002: Implementation of Activities and Use of Funds*. Geneva: the United Nations.

Powell, Colin. "US-China Relations," *South China Morning Post*, p. 17, February 28, 2003.

Shaughnessy, Edward L., ed. *China: The Land of the Heavenly Dragon*. London: Duncan Baird Publishers, 2000.

Sheff, David. *China Dawn: The Story of a Technology and Business Revolution*. New York: HarperBusiness, 2002.

Smith, Bradley and Wan-go Weng. *China: A History in Art*. New York: Harper & Row, 1973.

Stiglitz, Joseph and Shhid Yusuf, ed. *Rethinking the East Asian Miracle*. Washington DC: World Bank; Oxford: New York: Oxford University Press, 2001.

United Nations Educational, Scientific and Cultural Organization (UNESCO) and Organization for Economic Cooperation and Development (OECD). *Financing Education — Investments and Returns*. Paris: 2002.

Valder, Peter. *Gardens in China*. Portland, Oregon: Timber Press, 2002.

Young, Leslie. "The Tao of Markets: Sima Qian and the Invisible Hand." *Pacific Economic Review*, 1 (September 1996), pp. 137–45.

Yu, Ying-Shi. *Historical Study and Tradition* (*Shixue Yu Chuantong*, in Chinese). Taipei: China Times Press, 1981.

Index